D1014610

George W. Bush On God and Country

☆

Edited by Thomas M. Freiling

Allegiance Press, Inc.
WASHINGTON, D.C.

George W. Bush On God and Country
by Thomas M. Freiling

Printed in the United States of America

ISBN 1-591609-18-6

Allegiance Press
10640 Main Street
Suite 204
Fairfax, VA 22030

(703) 934-0173

☆

A charge to keep I have,
A God to glorify,
A never dying soul to save,
And fit it for the sky.
To serve the present age,
My calling to fulfill;
O may it all my powers engage
To do my Master's will!

—Charles Wesley

Contents

☆

Introduction

☆

Not since Abraham Lincoln has a sitting president talked so much about God as President George W. Bush. Ronald Reagan and Franklin Roosevelt referred to the Almighty on occasion too, but President Bush broaches spiritual issues with a frankness and conviction that is unprecedented in modern times.

President Bush discusses his faith — more specifically his Christian faith and America's religious roots — not only here at home, but overseas in meetings with world leaders. He talks about it in the context of domestic issues including abortion, AIDS, medical ethics, and social welfare. He even talks about it in terms of foreign policy, as he defends freedom and leads the fight against terrorism. Before running for president, as governor of Texas, he talked about the Creator during speeches and in rallies.

Why do we have to hearken back to the mid-nineteenth century to find a president willing to discuss his faith so openly? This book will help answer that question.

In my book, *Abraham Lincoln's Daily Treasure*, I give President Lincoln's moral and spiritual maxims. Lincoln prayed and read the Bible a lot during the dark day of the Civil War. His reliance on the Bible and his belief in Divine Providence inspired and united the country. "The Almighty has his own purposes," proclaimed Lincoln in his inaugural address, and "whatever shall appear to be God's will, I will do," as he emancipated the slaves.

In a similar manner, Bush finds direction and the source of his strength by calling on God's help. "When you realize that there is an Almighty God on whom you can rely, it provides great comfort," he once told Peggy Noonan, a former speechwriter for President Reagan.

Today, 150 years later in post-modern American, Bush's religious rhetoric has been the source of consternation for some. But I'm sure I speak for a vast majority of Americans that his words have been a source of encouragement and inspiration. They guide us toward the moral and spiritual foundations our country was founded upon.

President Bush's reverence for the Bible, his humble gratitude for our prayers, his respect for life based on God-given equal rights, his resolve to combat evil in the world, and his persistent calls for compassion, have revived America's soul and spirit. It has given us a renewed sense of our Divine Providence.

This book gives you a strong dose of President George W. Bush on God and country, stirring excerpts of the president's most important addresses and proclamations on issues that matter most to Americans who value faith and patriotism.

The idea for this book was conceived during a White House briefing I attended a few months after the horrific events of September 11, 2001. During the briefing some of the president's closest advisors gave an inside look into the life of the president. They told us how much he valued his faith — and how he relied on it for strength and direction during the days, weeks and months following the terror attacks on America.

Some of this I had already known. I had known about Bush's conversion to Christianity, about how Billy Graham helped him overcome his sinful nature, and about how he studied the Bible with his friend, Secretary of Commerce Don Evans. I had read how he begins each day in devotion, how he once called for an impromptu worship service aboard Air Force One, and how he had reportedly once prayed with British Prime Minister Tony Blair. But until that day, I did not fully appreciate the sincerity and depth of his convictions.

Maybe I had been a little swayed by the secular elite. The pundits, Hollywood actors, and university professors were saying Bush's spirituality was nothing more than politicking. They didn't believe he was "for real." They complained the president used the Oval Office as a "bully pulpit" and that he didn't tolerate divergent beliefs. The editorial page of *The New York Times* grumbled that Bush had been "referring to the Almighty so frequently that He is becoming his de facto running mate for 2004."

So after my visit to the White House, I set my course on setting the record straight. I was now convinced any criticism I heard was without merit. I researched every public address President George W. Bush gave about the role of religion in our government and society. Within these pages are what I found.

The Bible says out of the overflow of the heart, a man speaks. What did I find about what the president believes? What I found is a president who believes in the God of the Bible, and his son, Jesus Christ. He believes in the power of prayer, and that all men and women are created equal by God. He believes the Bible commands us to love our neighbor and have compassion. He believes that evil exists in the world, that freedom is our God-given right, and that as Americans we have a duty to protect the rights of all people to be free.

What I did not find — and what you *cannot* find if you try — is an intolerant and uncompassionate president. He goes to great lengths to define the limits of his public office, in terms of his faith-based principles. He uses the Bible and prayer to find comfort and help, not to condemn or discriminate. Most importantly, his religious beliefs are what drives his "compassionate conservative" polices on issues like AIDS and his faith-based initiatives to help the poor and needy.

Since President Bush's inaugural address in

2000, he has mentioned the Almighty in literally hundreds of speeches and proclamations. Of course I could not include them all here, so I selected the ones I believe to be the most important.

The materials herein collected were obtained from the official record of the White House. They are transcripts of the words as spoken by the president, not speeches to be read. They are excerpts, not complete transcripts. In most speeches, we eliminated the president's remarks thanking guests and other introductory comments. There were minor editorial changes. Some punctuation and misprints in the transcripts were corrected, and we removed "applause" and other reference to audience reactions.

I saved the dedication page of this book to give you President Bush's favorite hymn, called "A Charge to Keep," written by Methodist minister Charles Wesley. They hymn also inspired a painting which hangs in the Oval Office. As governor of Texas, Bush sent a memo to his staff, "When you come into my office, please take a look at the beautiful painting of a horseman determinedly charging up what appears to be a steep and rough trail. This is us. What adds complete life to the painting for me is the message of Charles Wesley that we serve One greater than ourselves." Bush goes on to say, "A charge to keep calls us to our highest and best. It speaks of purpose and direction." The hymn is often associated with a Bible verse, I Corinthians 4:2, *"Now it is required that those who have been given a trust must prove faithful."*

Those who deserve thanks for their help on this

book include my hard-working staff, Debbie Lewis, Kathy Curtis, and Cathy Gilstrap. I would also like to thank Larry Carpenter and Dave Troutman for their help in taking the words in this book to readers through bookstores and libraries.

—Thomas M. Freiling

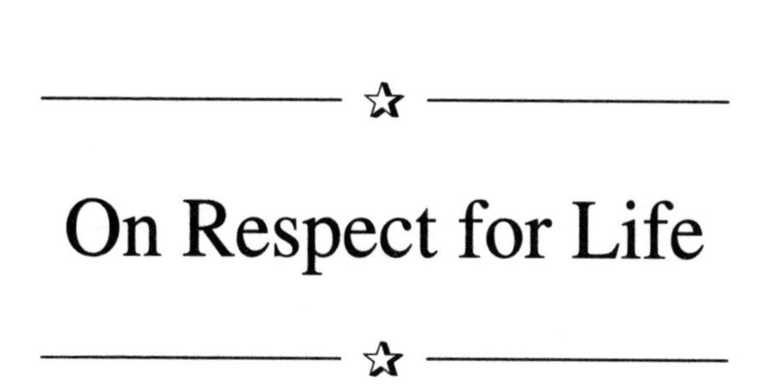

On Respect for Life

I worry about a culture that devalues life, and believe as your president I have an important obligation to foster and encourage respect for life in America and throughout the world.
–AUGUST 9, 2001

The issue of research involving stem cells derived from human embryos is increasingly the subject of a national debate and dinner table discussions. The issue is confronted every day in laboratories as scientists ponder the ethical ramifications of their work. It is agonized over by parents and many couples as they try to have children, or to save children already born.

The issue is debated within the church, with people of different faiths, even many of the same faith coming to different conclusions. Many people are finding that the more they know about stem cell research, the less certain they are about the right ethical and moral conclusions.

My administration must decide whether to allow federal funds, your tax dollars, to be used for scientific research on stem cells derived from human embryos. A large number of these embryos already exist. They are the product of a process called in vitro fertilization, which helps so many couples conceive children. When doctors match sperm and egg to create life outside the womb, they usually produce more embryos than are planted in the mother. Once a couple successfully has children, or if they are unsuccessful, the additional embryos remain frozen in laboratories.

Some will not survive during long storage; others are destroyed. A number have been donated to science and used to create privately funded stem cell lines. And a few have been implanted in an adoptive mother and born, and are today healthy children.

Based on preliminary work that has been privately funded, scientists believe further research using stem cells offers great promise that could help improve the lives of those who suffer from many terrible diseases — from juvenile diabetes to Alzheimer's, from Parkinson's to spinal cord injuries. And while scientists admit they are not yet certain, they believe stem cells derived from embryos have unique potential.

You should also know that stem cells can be derived from sources other than embryos — from adult cells, from umbilical cords that are discarded after babies are born, from human placenta. And many scientists feel research on these type of stem cells is also promising. Many patients suffering from a range of diseases are already being helped with treatments developed from adult stem cells.

However, most scientists, at least today, believe

that research on embryonic stem cells offer the most promise because these cells have the potential to develop in all of the tissues in the body.

Scientists further believe that rapid progress in this research will come only with federal funds. Federal dollars help attract the best and brightest scientists. They ensure new discoveries are widely shared at the largest number of research facilities and that the research is directed toward the greatest public good.

The United States has a long and proud record of leading the world toward advances in science and medicine that improve human life. And the United States has a long and proud record of upholding the highest standards of ethics as we expand the limits of science and knowledge. Research on embryonic stem cells raises profound ethical questions, because extracting the stem cell destroys the embryo, and thus destroys its potential for life. Like a snowflake, each of these embryos is unique, with the unique genetic potential of an individual human being.

As I thought through this issue, I kept returning to two fundamental questions: First, are these frozen embryos human life, and therefore, something precious to be protected? And second, if they're going to be destroyed anyway, shouldn't they be used for a greater good, for research that has the potential to save and improve other lives?

I've asked those questions and others of scientists, scholars, bioethicists, religious leaders, doctors, researchers, members of Congress, my Cabinet, and my friends. I have read heartfelt letters from many

Americans. I have given this issue a great deal of thought, prayer and considerable reflection. And I have found widespread disagreement.

On the first issue, are these embryos human life — well, one researcher told me he believes this five-day-old cluster of cells is not an embryo, not yet an individual, but a pre-embryo. He argued that it has the potential for life, but it is not a life because it cannot develop on its own.

An ethicist dismissed that as a callous attempt at rationalization. Make no mistake, he told me, that cluster of cells is the same way you and I, and all the rest of us, started our lives. One goes with a heavy heart if we use these, he said, because we are dealing with the seeds of the next generation.

And to the other crucial question, if these are going to be destroyed anyway, why not use them for good purpose — I also found different answers. Many argue these embryos are byproducts of a process that helps create life, and we should allow couples to donate them to science so they can be used for good purpose instead of wasting their potential. Others will argue there's no such thing as excess life, and the fact that a living being is going to die does not justify experimenting on it or exploiting it as a natural resource.

At its core, this issue forces us to confront fundamental questions about the beginnings of life and the ends of science. It lies at a difficult moral intersection, juxtaposing the need to protect life in all its phases with the prospect of saving and improving life in all its stages.

As the discoveries of modern science create tremendous hope, they also lay vast ethical mine fields. As the genius of science extends the horizons of what we can do, we increasingly confront complex questions about what we should do. We have arrived at that brave new world that seemed so distant in 1932, when Aldous Huxley wrote about human beings created in test tubes in what he called a "hatchery."

In recent weeks, we learned that scientists have created human embryos in test tubes solely to experiment on them. This is deeply troubling, and a warning sign that should prompt all of us to think through these issues very carefully.

Embryonic stem cell research is at the leading edge of a series of moral hazards. The initial stem cell researcher was at first reluctant to begin his research, fearing it might be used for human cloning. Scientists have already cloned a sheep. Researchers are telling us the next step could be to clone human beings to create individual designer stem cells, essentially to grow another you, to be available in case you need another heart or lung or liver.

I strongly oppose human cloning, as do most Americans. We recoil at the idea of growing human beings for spare body parts, or creating life for our convenience. And while we must devote enormous energy to conquering disease, it is equally important that we pay attention to the moral concerns raised by the new frontier of human embryo stem cell research. Even the most noble ends do not justify any means.

My position on these issues is shaped by deeply

held beliefs. I'm a strong supporter of science and technology, and believe they have the potential for incredible good — to improve lives, to save life, to conquer disease. Research offers hope that millions of our loved ones may be cured of a disease and rid of their suffering. I have friends whose children suffer from juvenile diabetes. Nancy Reagan has written me about President Reagan's struggle with Alzheimer's. My own family has confronted the tragedy of childhood leukemia. And, like all Americans, I have great hope for cures.

I also believe human life is a sacred gift from our Creator. I worry about a culture that devalues life, and believe as your president I have an important obligation to foster and encourage respect for life in America and throughout the world. And while we're all hopeful about the potential of this research, no one can be certain that the science will live up to the hope it has generated.

Eight years ago, scientists believed fetal tissue research offered great hope for cures and treatments — yet, the progress to date has not lived up to its initial expectations. Embryonic stem cell research offers both great promise and great peril. So I have decided we must proceed with great care.

As a result of private research, more than 60 genetically diverse stem cell lines already exist. They were created from embryos that have already been destroyed, and they have the ability to regenerate themselves indefinitely, creating ongoing opportunities for research. I have concluded that we should allow federal funds to be used for research on these existing stem cell lines, where the life and death decision has already been made.

Leading scientists tell me research on these 60 lines has great promise that could lead to breakthrough therapies and cures. This allows us to explore the promise and potential of stem cell research without crossing a fundamental moral line, by providing taxpayer funding that would sanction or encourage further destruction of human embryos that have at least the potential for life.

I also believe that great scientific progress can be made through aggressive federal funding of research on umbilical cord placenta, adult and animal stem cells which do not involve the same moral dilemma. This year, your government will spend $250 million on this important research.

I will also name a president's council to monitor stem cell research, to recommend appropriate guidelines and regulations, and to consider all of the medical and ethical ramifications of biomedical innovation. This council will consist of leading scientists, doctors, ethicists, lawyers, theologians and others, and will be chaired by Dr. Leon Kass, a leading biomedical ethicist from the University of Chicago.

This council will keep us apprised of new developments and give our nation a forum to continue to discuss and evaluate these important issues. As we go forward, I hope we will always be guided by both intellect and heart, by both our capabilities and our conscience.

I have made this decision with great care, and I

pray it is the right one.

Thank you for listening. Good night, and God bless America.

On Compassionate Conservatism

Our nation is unique in this way: We are a nation of people who have heard a call to love a neighbor.
–MAY 22, 2001

My vision includes everybody. It's described as compassionate conservatism, but I emphasize the compassion. The problem is government is not a very compassionate organization. We can fund — and we should — budgets, there is a lot of talk about budgets. We've submitted budgets that increase spending on social services. We've got what's called a compassion fund, that matches — a $500 million-dollar fund that will encourage faith-based initiatives throughout the country.

But the dilemma and the problem in the past has been that somewhere along the line everybody thought government could make people love one another. And that's not the way it works. And if part of the future of the country is to love a neighbor like you would like to be loved yourself, it seems to follow then our government must welcome, not discriminate against, faith-based organizations who are providing that.

I hope the Congress does not get caught up in the stale, old process argument of the legalisms involved with encouraging organizations of faith to help people in need. Because as Louise mentioned, there is precedent. We fund religious hospitals through Medicare and Medicaid. There is scholarship money for children to use at religious institutions.

Why does it not follow, I asked the Congress and those folks elected, that we not allow faith-based programs to compete for taxpayers' money if the services they provide are necessary and the results are positive? The argument is, let us focus on the process. We're saying, let us focus on the results.

The way I like to put it — I gave a speech at Notre Dame last Sunday, it was a speech that said, it started with talking about President Lyndon Johnson's speech at the University of Texas, kicking off the war on poverty. It recognized that that war on poverty had some positive effects. It also recognized, though, it had created a dependency on government. It had a perverse effect.

So then the welfare law came along in 1996, signed by my predecessor, it had bipartisan support, that tried to address the concept of dependency upon government. But we need to take it a step further, because there are still people who hurt and people whose lives are affected, people whose hearts need mending. Government must be active to fund the services, but humble to recognize the power of neighborhood healers and helpers; humble to step aside when somebody can do a better job.

I've been so impressed by the faith-based leaders

I've met all around our country, because there is a genuine commitment to the poor and the disadvantaged. And that's a commitment that we must channel and a commitment we must harvest. I used to say in the campaign, I look forward to rallying the soldiers and the armies of compassion. And I mean that.

Our nation is so unique in this way: we are a nation of people who have heard a call to love a neighbor. We really are. I was sharing with the good leaders that came to visit me about the fact that everywhere I go people say, Mr. President, I'm praying for you. They're not saying it's a Democrat prayer or a Republican prayer. It's just prayer.

It reminds me on a daily basis about the great hope and promise of America. It also reminds me how lucky I am to be the president of a great land, where people truly care about our country. It also reminds me about what government ought to do. We ought to set money out there to encourage faith-based initiatives.

At the same time, we must never be so arrogant as to say, you can't fulfill your mission if you access federal money, therefore, you have to change the entire mission of why you exist. I understand the frustrations with some in the faith-based community, and the nervousness as they approach this issue. They say to themselves, why would I want to access federal money if the federal government then tries to take away my mission, to take the cross off the wall or the Star of David off the wall? Why would I want to interface with a government that's going to say, we'll reluctantly give you money, and then force you to change your calling?

Well, I can understand that. And one of our commitments is that we will work tirelessly to make sure that bureaucracies don't stifle the very reason you exist in the first place, and the power of your ministries, which is faith — which is faith.

And so my message to you is thanks for what you're doing. You'll have a friend and an advocate in this administration that marches side-by-side — side-by side; that we will do our very level best to make sure that the bureaucratic obstacles are cleared and that people in need are able to get help.

In the course of the campaign I tried to explain what a faith-based initiative meant to many members of the press that followed me and, of course, many citizens. I'll never forget going to Colfax, Iowa for a teen challenge program. You know, sometimes people accuse me of not being very articulate. English is my second language. But there was nothing more articulate than seeing a person who had been hooked on serious drugs stand up and explain to the nation — at least those willing to listen — how he kicked drugs because faith had entered into his life.

It's hard to measure that. There is no formula for that. You can't write a regulation or a bureaucratic rule that suggests that that happen. But what government can do is recognize its limitations and, more significantly, recognize the power of faith in our society. And that's what this initiative does. We don't pick religions, we don't fund religion. But we welcome the soldiers of the armies of compassion.

And to you soldiers, thank you so much for being here, thank you for caring about our great land and thank you for the service you provide on a daily basis.

God bless.

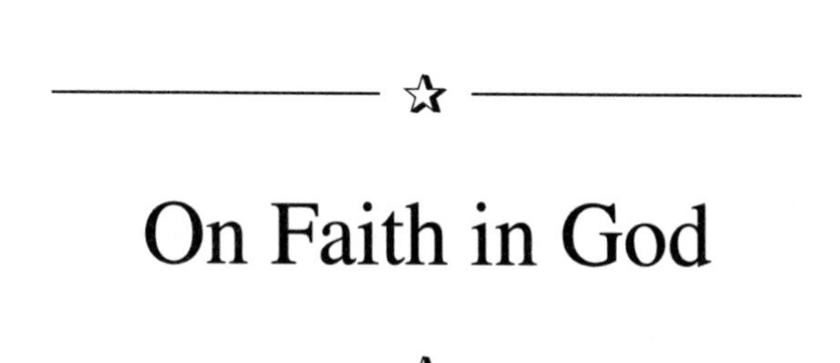

On Faith in God

Once we have recognized God's image in ourselves, we must recognize it in every human being.
–FEBRUARY 7, 2002

Since we met last year, millions of Americans have been led to prayer. They have prayed for comfort in time of grief; for understanding in a time of anger; for protection in a time of uncertainty. Many, including me, have been on bended knee. The prayers of this nation are a part of the good that has come from the evil of September the 11th, more good than we could ever have predicted. Tragedy has brought forth the courage and the generosity of our people.

None of us would ever wish on anyone what happened on that day. Yet, as with each life, sorrows we would not choose can bring wisdom and strength gained in no other way. This insight is central to many faiths, and certainly to faith that finds hope and comfort in a cross.

Every religion is welcomed in our country; all are practiced here. Many of our good citizens profess no religion at all. Our country has never had an official faith. Yet we have all been witnesses these past 21 weeks to the power of faith to see us through the hurt and loss that has come to our country.

Faith gives the assurance that our lives and our history have a moral design. As individuals, we know that suffering is temporary, and hope is eternal. As a nation, we know that the ruthless will not inherit the Earth. Faith teaches humility, and with it, tolerance. Once we have recognized God's image in ourselves, we must recognize it in every human being.

Respect for the dignity of others can be found outside of religion, just as intolerance is sometimes found within it. Yet for millions of Americans, the practice of tolerance is a command of faith. When our country was attacked, Americans did not respond with bigotry. People from other countries and cultures have been treated with respect. And this is one victory in the war against terror.

At the same time, faith shows us the reality of good, and the reality of evil. Some acts and choices in this world have eternal consequences. It is always, and everywhere, wrong to target and kill the innocent. It is always, and everywhere, wrong to be cruel and hateful, to enslave and oppress. It is always, and everywhere, right to be kind and just, to protect the lives of others, and to lay down your life for a friend.

The men and women who charged into burning buildings to save others, those who fought the hijackers, were not confused about the difference between right and wrong. They knew the difference. They knew their duty. And we know their sacrifice was not in vain.

Faith shows us the way to self-giving, to love our neighbor as we would want to be loved ourselves. In service to others, we find deep human fulfillment. And as acts of service are multiplied, our nation becomes a more welcoming place for the weak, and a better place for those who suffer and grieve.

For half a century now, the National Prayer Breakfast has been a symbol of the vital place of faith in the life of our nation. You've reminded generations of leaders of a purpose and a power greater than their own. In times of calm, and in times of crisis, you've called us to prayer.

In this time of testing for our nation, my family and I have been blessed by the prayers of countless of Americans. We have felt their sustaining power and we're incredibly grateful. Tremendous challenges await this nation, and there will be hardships ahead. Faith will not make our path easy, but it will give us strength for the journey.

The promise of faith is not the absence of suffering; it is the presence of grace. And at every step we are secure in knowing that suffering produces perseverance, and perseverance produces character, and character produces hope — and hope does not disappoint.

May God bless you, and may God continue to bless America.

On Hope

Hope allows us to dream big, to pray bold,
and to work hard for a better future.
–May 15, 2003

☆

It is important, and it is good to begin the day with prayer and fellowship. Prayer is an opportunity to praise God for His works and to thank Him for His blessings. Prayer turns our minds to the needs of others, and prayer changes our hearts as we seek God's will.

I want to thank you for reminding the nation, and our capital, about an even greater source of strength and authority.

Last May, when I came, you honored me with a special gift, a bilingual Bible that was made for me in Mexico. And this Bible means a lot because with it came a promise. You promised that you were praying for me. There is no greater gift that a president can receive. I have felt the comfort of those prayers. And I am really grateful. Thank you, from the bottom of my heart.

Hispanic Americans bring many gifts to this nation — hard work and strong cultural traditions and patriotism. Above all, the Hispanic community lives every day por los valores de fe y familia. Your good works and reverence bring compassion to our country, and honor to almighty God.

In the last several weeks, we have learned the names of some exceptional young men and women who have shown the strength and character of America. At the National Naval Medical Center, I met Master Gunnery Sergeant Guadalupe Denogean. Sergeant Denogean is an immigrant from Mexico who served in the Marine Corps for 25 years. This spring he was wounded near Basra, and he was sent back to America for treatment. When asked if he had any requests, the good Sergeant just had two — a promotion for the corporal who helped rescue him, and he wanted to be an American citizen.

I was honored to be with the Sergeant the day he received a Purple Heart and took the oath of citizenship. It was an amazing experience, a truly American experience, to be in the hospital where he was recovering from his wound; to see this son of Mexico raise his right hand and pledge to support and defend the Constitution of the United States. He had kept that oath for decades before he took it. And I'm proud to call him my fellow American.

Our country is proud of all the Hispanic Americans who serve in uniform. We're deeply grateful for those who have died in the cause of our security, and in the cause of freedom. We honor their memory. We pray for their families. We honor the communities and the churches where they learn the value of service and sacrifice.

Because of their sacrifices, America is a more

secure country. Because of their sacrifices, the world will be a more peaceful place. And because of their sacrifices, people who had lived in bondage under the strong arm of a brutal dictator are now free.

America is blessed by their sacrifices. And America is also blessed by the sacrifices that you make every day as you care for the sick, house the homeless, feed the hungry, and preach the word — la palabra.

In the Book of James, we are reminded that faith without works is dead. By loving a neighbor as you'd like to be loved yourself, you prove every day that faith is alive. By your work and prayers, you have formed your own army, an army of compassion. And by living your faith, you bring hope to those who need it most.

It is appropriate that the group sponsoring this breakfast has the name Nueva Esperanza — New Hope. Hope allows us to dream big, to pray bold, and to work hard for a better future. I want to thank you for your abiding hope, for your steadfast faith, and for your acts of love. I want to thank you for helping to keep prayer an important part of our national life. May God continue to invigorate you as you work to make this country a compassionate home for anybody. May God continue to invigorate you as you reach out to help a neighbor in need.

This country needs your compassion. We need your works. We need your love. May God bless you all, and may God continue to bless America.

On God's Blessings

In the aftermath of the attacks, the words of the Psalms brought comfort to many. We trust God always to be our refuge and our strength, an ever-present help in time of trouble.
–AUGUST 31, 2002

As we remember the tragic events of September 11, 2001, and the thousands of innocent lives lost on that day, we recall as well the outpouring of compassion and faith that swept our Nation in the face of the evil done that day. In designating September 6-8 as National Days of Prayer and Remembrance, I ask all Americans to join together in cities, communities, neighborhoods, and places of worship to honor those who were lost, to pray for those who grieve, and to give thanks for God's enduring blessings on our land. And let us, through prayer, seek the wisdom, patience, and strength to bring those responsible for the attacks to justice and to press for a world at peace.

For the families and friends of those who died, each new day has required new courage. Their perseverance has touched us deeply, and their noble character has brought us hope. We stand with them in faith, and we cherish with them the memory of those who perished.

In the aftermath of the attacks, the words of the Psalms brought comfort to many. We trust God always to be our refuge and our strength, an ever-present help in time of trouble. Believing that One greater than ourselves watches over our lives and over this Nation, we continue to place our trust in Him.

The events of September 11 altered our lives, the life of this Nation, and the world. Americans responded to terror with resolve and determination, first recovering, now rebuilding, and, at all times, committing ourselves to protecting our people and preserving our freedom. And we have found hope and healing in our faith, families, and friendships. As we confront the challenges before us, I ask you to join me during these Days of Prayer and Remembrance in praying for God's continued protection and for the strength to overcome great evil with even greater good.

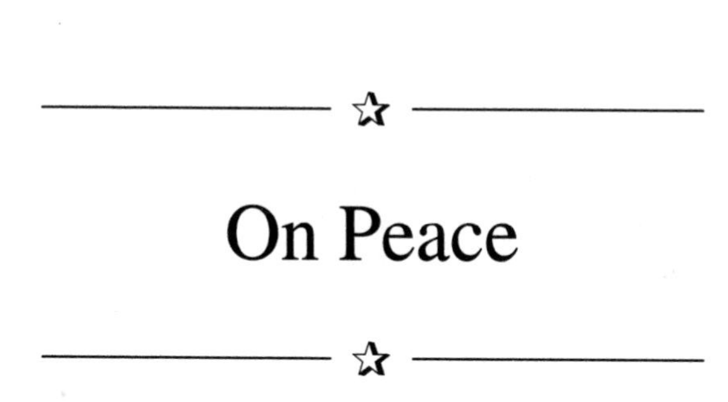

On Peace

In these extraordinary times, our Nation has once again been challenged, and Lincoln's words remain our guiding prayer.
–MAY 21, 2002

☆

Every Memorial Day, Americans remember the debt of gratitude we owe to our veterans who gave their lives for our country. On this important day, communities across our Nation stop to remember and to honor the great sacrifices made by our men and women in uniform.

Since its beginnings, our country has faced many threats that have tested its courage. From war-torn battlefields and jungle skirmishes to conflicts at sea and air attacks, generations of brave men and women have fought and died to defeat tyranny and protect our democracy. Their sacrifices have made this Nation strong and our world a better place.

Upwards of 48 million Americans have served the cause of freedom and more than a million have died to preserve our liberty. We also remember the more than 140,000 who were taken prisoner-of-war and the many others who were never accounted for. These memories remind us that the cost of war and the price of peace are great.

The tradition of Memorial Day reinforces our Nation's resolve to never forget those who gave their last full measure for America. As we engage in the war against terrorism, we also pray for peace. When America emerged from the Civil War, President Abraham Lincoln called on all Americans to "cherish a just and lasting peace." In these extraordinary times, our Nation has once again been challenged, and Lincoln's words remain our guiding prayer.

We continue to rely on our brave and steadfast men and women in uniform to defend our freedom. United as a people, we pray for peace throughout the world. We also pray for the safety of our troops. This new generation follows an unbroken line of good, courageous, and unfaltering heroes who have never let our country down.

As we commemorate this noble American holiday, we honor those who fell in defense of freedom. We honor them in our memory through solemn observances, with the love of a grateful Nation.

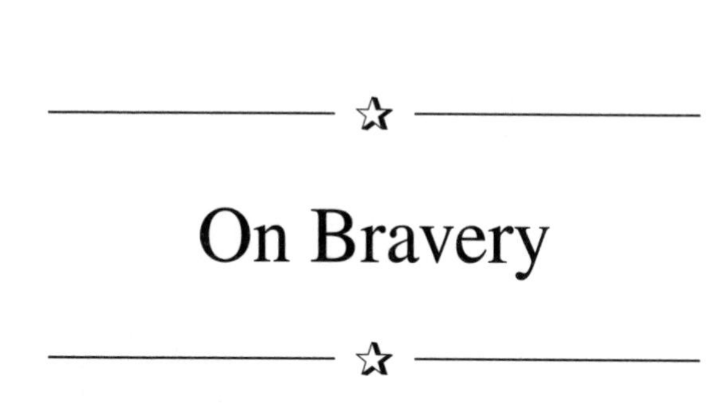

On Bravery

America, he said, has sent the best of her young men around the world, not to conquer, but to liberate; not to terrorize, but to help.
–NOVEMBER 11, 2001

☆

The evil ones have roused a mighty nation, a mighty land. And for however long it takes, I am determined that we will prevail. And prevail we must, because we fight for one thing, and that is the freedom of our people, and the freedom of people everywhere.

And I want to thank the Commissioner, who is a veteran as well — a veteran in the military, and a veteran of a new kind of war, one fought here on the home front. He represents the fabulous men and women who wear the uniform of the police and fire and rescue units, the Port Authority here in New York City, people who serve with such distinction and such courage that whenever an American hears the word police or fire we think differently. We think differently about the job. We think differently about the character of those who serve on a daily basis. We think differently about those who go to work every single day to protect us and save us and comfort us.

And in a time of war, we look a little differently at our veterans, too. We pay tributes on Veterans Day, today, and they're made with a little greater feeling, because Americans have seen the terrible harm that an enemy can inflict. And it has left us deeply grateful for the men and women who rise strongly in the defense of our nation. We appreciate the sacrifices that our military is making today. We appreciate the sacrifices that their families make with them.

When the call comes to defend our country, our military is ready, and is making us proud. Al Qaeda and the Taliban have made a serious mistake. And because our military is brave and prepared and courageous, they will pay a serious price.

America has always needed such bravery and such people, and we have always found them amongst us. Generations of our servicemen and women have not only fought for our country in the past, they have upheld our honorable traditions, and represented our country with courage and honor. And wherever our military has gone, they have brought pride to our own people and hope to millions of others.

One veteran of World War II recalled the spirit of the American military and the relief it brought to suffering peoples. America, he said, has sent the best of her young men around the world, not to conquer, but to liberate; not to terrorize, but to help.

And this is true in Afghanistan today. And this has always been true of the men and women who have served our nation. This nation is freedom's home, and freedom's defender. And we owe so much — so much — to the men and women, our veterans, who step forward to protect those freedoms.

Our veterans gave America some of the best years of their lives, and stood ready to give life itself. For all that, America's 25 million veterans have the deep respect of their fellow citizens, and the enduring gratitude of a nation they so nobly served.

May God bless our veterans, and may God continue to bless America.

On Human Dignity

Every child is a priority and a blessing,
and I believe that all should be welcomed
in life and protected by law.
–JANUARY 14, 2003

Our nation was built on a promise of life and liberty for all citizens. Guided by a deep respect for human dignity, our Founding Fathers worked to secure these rights for future generations, and today we continue to seek to fulfill their promise in our laws and our society. On National Sanctity of Human Life Day, we reaffirm the value of human life and renew our dedication to ensuring that every American has access to life, liberty, and the pursuit of happiness.

As we seek to improve quality of life, overcome illness, and promote vital medical research, my Administration will continue to honor our country's founding ideals of equal dignity and equal rights for every American. Every child is a priority and a blessing, and I believe that all should be welcomed in life and protected by law. My Administration has championed compassionate alternatives to abortion, such as helping women in crisis through maternity group homes, encouraging adoption, promoting abstinence education, and passing laws requiring parental notification and waiting periods for minors.

The Born-Alive Infants Protection Act, which I signed into law in August 2002, is an important contribution to our efforts to care for human life. This important legislation helps protect the most vulnerable members of our society by ensuring that every infant born alive, including one who survives abortion, is considered a person and receives protection under Federal law. It helps achieve the promises of the Declaration of Independence for all, including those without the voice and power to defend their own rights.

Through ethical policies and the compassion of Americans, we will continue to build a culture that respects life. Faith-based and community organizations and individual citizens play a critical role in strengthening our neighborhoods and bringing care and comfort to those in need. By helping fellow citizens, these groups recognize the dignity of every human being and the possibilities of every life; and their important efforts are helping to build a more just and generous Nation. By working together to protect the weak, the imperfect, and the unwanted, we affirm a culture of hope and help ensure a brighter future for all.

On the Right to Life

Unborn children should be welcomed in life
and protected in law.
–JANUARY 18, 2002

This Nation was founded upon the belief that every human being is endowed by our Creator with certain "unalienable rights." Chief among them is the right to life itself. The Signers of the Declaration of Independence pledged their own lives, fortunes, and honor to guarantee inalienable rights for all of the new country's citizens. These visionaries recognized that an essential human dignity attached to all persons by virtue of their very existence and not just to the strong, the independent, or the healthy. That value should apply to every American, including the elderly and the unprotected, the weak and the infirm, and even to the unwanted.

Thomas Jefferson wrote that, "[t]he care of human life and happiness and not their destruction is the first and only legitimate object of good government." President Jefferson was right. Life is an inalienable right, understood as given to each of us by our Creator.

President Jefferson's timeless principle obligates us to pursue a civil society that will democratically embrace its essential moral duties, including defending the elderly, strengthening the weak, protecting the defenseless, feeding the hungry, and caring for children — born and unborn. Mindful of these and other obligations, we should join together in pursuit of a more compassionate society, rejecting the notion that some lives are less worthy of protection than others, whether because of age or illness, social circumstance or economic condition. Consistent with the core principles about which Thomas Jefferson wrote, and to which the Founders subscribed, we should peacefully commit ourselves to seeking a society that values life — from its very beginnings to its natural end. Unborn children should be welcomed in life and protected in law.

On September 11, we saw clearly that evil exists in this world, and that it does not value life. The terrible events of that fateful day have given us, as a Nation, a greater understanding about the value and wonder of life. Every innocent life taken that day was the most important person on earth to somebody; and every death extinguished a world. Now we are engaged in a fight against evil and tyranny to preserve and protect life. In so doing, we are standing again for those core principles upon which our Nation was founded.

On Prayer in American History

So many great events in our nation's history were shaped by men and women who found strength and direction in prayer.
–May 1, 2003

So many great events in our nation's history were shaped by men and women who found strength and direction in prayer. The first president to live in this house composed a prayer on his second evening here for all who would follow him. Our 16th president, Abraham Lincoln, knew that his burdens were too great for any man, so he carried them to God in prayer. Over the radio on D-Day in 1944, Franklin Roosevelt prayed for God's blessing on our mission to "set free a suffering humanity."

This past month has been another time of testing for America and another time of intense prayer. Americans have been praying for the safety of our troops and for the protection of innocent life in Iraq. Americans prayed that war would not be necessary, and now pray that peace will be just and lasting.

We continue to pray for the recovery of the

wounded and for the comfort of all who have lost a loved one. The Scriptures say: the Lord is near to all who call on him. Calling on God in prayer brings us nearer to each other. After his son was rescued from northern Iraq, the father of Sergeant James Riley of New Jersey said, "We have been flooded with people's prayers. Everyone is praying for us and we are so grateful."

During Operation Iraqi Freedom, many Americans have registered online to adopt a serviceman or woman in prayer. Others wear prayer bracelets to remind themselves to intercede on behalf of our troops. In Fountain City, Wisconsin, Lynn Cox has collected at least 80 Bibles to send to those serving in Iraq. In Green, Ohio, a group of parishioners at Queen of Heaven Catholic Church has made 2,000 rosaries for our troops. Margaret Brown, who helped start the group, said, "We want them to know that someone back here is holding them up in prayer, and that God is so powerful He can supply all their needs."

To pray for someone else is an act of generosity. We set our own cares aside and look to strengthen another. Prayer teaches humility. We find that the plan of the Creator is sometimes very different from our own. Yet, we learn to depend on His loving will, bowing to purposes we don't always understand. Prayer can lead to a grateful heart, turning our minds to all the gifts of life and to the great works of God.

Prayer can also contribute to the life of our nation. America is a strong nation, in part because we know the limits of human strength. All strength must be guided by wisdom and justice and humility. We pray that God will grant us that wisdom, that sense of justice and that humility in our current challenges, and in the years ahead.

I thank you all for helping to keep prayer an integral part of our national life. May God bless each one of you, and may God continue to bless the United States of America.

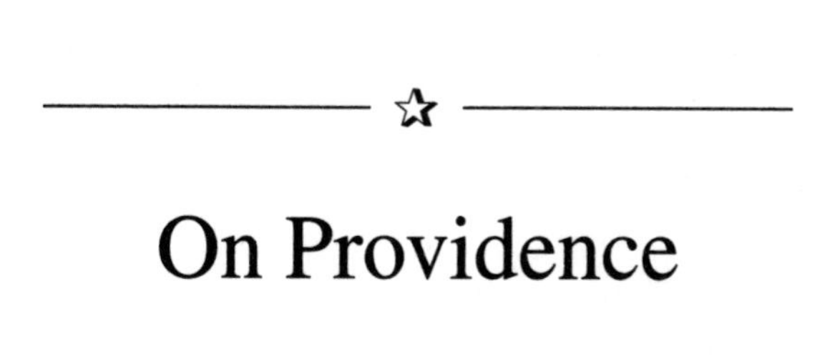

On Providence

Behind all of life and all of history,
there's a dedication and purpose,
set by the hand of a just and faithful God.
–February 6, 2003

I know, from firsthand knowledge, that this is a nation of prayer. See, I work the ropelines a lot, and I hear all kinds of things on the ropelines. But the thing I hear the most, the comment I hear the most from our fellow citizens, regardless of their political party or philosophy, is, Mr. President, I pray for you and your family, and so does my family. That's what I hear. I turn to them without hesitation and say, it is the greatest gift you can give anybody, is to pray on their behalf.

I especially feel that because I believe in prayer. I pray. I pray for strength, I pray for guidance, I pray for forgiveness. And I pray to offer my thanks for a kind and generous Almighty God.

As Dick mentioned, we mourn the loss of seven brave souls. We learned a lot about them over the last couple of days, and Laura and I learned a lot about their families in Houston, because we met with them. My impressions of the meeting was that there was — that Almighty God was present in their hearts. There was such incredible strength in the room of those who were grieving that it was overwhelming, to be with those who just lost their husband or wife or dad or mom, and to feel the presence of the Almighty. I attribute it to the fact that they, themselves, are in prayer. And our country prays for their strength. And we must continue to pray for those who suffer and those who grieve.

This is a testing time for our country. At this hour we have troops that are assembling in the Middle East. There's oppressive regimes that seek terrible weapons. We face an ongoing threat of terror. One thing is for certain: we didn't ask for these challenges, but we will meet them. I say that with certainty, because this nation has strong foundations that won't be shaken.

As America passes through this decisive period, there are things we can count on. We can be confident in the character of the American people. The months since September the 11th, 2001, have not brought fear and fatigue or rash anger. Instead we've witnessed courage and resolve and calm purpose. We've seen that a new generation of Americans is strong and steadfast in the face of danger, and our confidence will not be shaken.

We can be confident in America's cause in the world. Our nation is dedicated to the equal and undeniable worth of every person. We don't own the ideals of freedom and human dignity, and sometimes we haven't always lived up to them. But we do stand for those ideals, and we will defend them.

We believe, as Franklin Roosevelt said, that men and women born to freedom in the image of God will not forever suffer the oppressor's sword. We are confident that people in every part of the world wish for freedom, not tyranny; or for peace to terror and violence. And our confidence will not be shaken.

We can also be confident in the ways of Providence, even when they are far from our understanding. Events aren't moved by blind change and chance. Behind all of life and all of history, there's a dedication and purpose, set by the hand of a just and faithful God. And that hope will never be shaken.

In this hour of our country's history, we stand in the need of prayer. We pray for the families that have known recent loss. We pray for the men and women who serve around the world to defend our freedom. We pray for their families. We pray for wisdom to know and do what is right. And we pray for God's peace in the affairs of men.

May God bless you all.

On Church and State

True faith is never isolated from the rest of life,
and faith without works is dead.
–JUNE 11, 2002

Thank you all very much. Dr. Merritt, thanks so much. It's good to be able to see you via video. I want to thank you for coming to the White House right after September the 11th, and thank you for such a kind introduction. I appreciate your friendship, and I'm honored to join all of you for the 2002 Southern Baptist Convention Annual Meeting. And I'm grateful for the opportunity to address you on this most special occasion.

As you gather this week in St. Louis, you'll choose a new president, and you will renew old and honorable commitments. Three centuries ago, there were fewer than 500 Baptists in America. Today, there are almost 16 million members of the Southern Baptist Convention. From your denomination have come presidents like Harry Truman and preachers like Roger Williams and Billy Graham, a man who has played such an important role in nurturing my faith.

Baptists have had an extraordinary influence on American history. They were among the earliest champions of religious tolerance and freedom. Baptists have long upheld the ideal of a free church in a free state. And from the beginning, they believed that forcing a person to worship against his will violated the principles of both Christianity and civility.

What I found interesting is the Baptist form of church government was a model of democracy even before the founding of America. And Baptists understood the deep truth of what Reverend Martin Luther King, Jr., said: "The church is not the master or the servant of the state, but rather the conscience of the state."

Since the earliest days of our Republic, Baptists have been guardians of the separation of church and state, preserving the integrity of both. Yet, you have never believed in separating religious faith from political life. Baptists believe as America's founders did: that religious faith is the moral anchor of American life.

Throughout history, people of faith have often been our nation's voice of conscience. We all know that men and women can be good without faith. And we also know that faith is an incredibly important source of goodness in our country.

True faith is never isolated from the rest of life, and faith without works is dead. Our democratic government is one way to promote social justice and the common good, which is why the Southern Baptist Convention has become a powerful voice for some of the great issues of our time.

You and I share common commitments. We believe in fostering a culture of life, and that marriage and family are sacred institutions that should be preserved and strengthened. We believe that a life is a creation, not a commodity, and that our children are gifts to be loved and protected, not products to be designed and manufactured by human cloning.

We believe that protecting human dignity and promoting human rights should be at the center of America's foreign policy. We believe that our government should view the good people who work in faith-based charities as partners, not rivals. We believe that the days of discriminating against religious institutions simply because they are religious must come to an end.

Faith teaches us to respect those with whom we disagree. It teaches us to tolerate one another. And it teaches us that the proper way to treat human beings created in the divine image is with civility. Yet, you also know that civility does not require us to abandon deeply held beliefs. Civility and firm resolve can live easily with one another.

Faith teaches us that God has a special concern for the poor, and that faith proves itself through actions and sacrifice, through acts of kindness and caring for those in need. For some people, Jesus' admonition to care "for the least of these" is an admirable moral teaching. For many Baptists, it is a way of life.

Faith is also a source of comfort during times of

grief. We saw this in the aftermath of the attacks on September the 11th. Millions of Americans turned to prayer for wisdom and resolve, for compassion and courage, and for grace and mercy. And in these moments of prayer, we are reminded of important truths: that suffering is temporary, that hope is eternal, and that the ruthless will not inherit the earth.

Our faith teaches us that while weeping may endure for a night, joy comes in the morning. And while faith will not make our path easy, it will give us strength for the journey ahead.

Many of you have prayed for my family and me. We have felt sustained and uplifted by your prayers. Laura and I are incredibly grateful to you for those prayers. We consider your prayers to be a most precious gift.

I want to thank you all for your good works. You're believers, and you're patriots, faithful followers of God and good citizens of America. And one day, I believe that it will be said of you, "Well done, good and faithful servants."

May God bless you all, and may God continue to bless America.

On War

And in all those victories American soldiers came to liberate, not to conquer.
–May 27, 2003

☆

We have gathered on this quiet corner of France as the sun rises on Memorial Day in the United States of America. This is a day our country has set apart to remember what was gained in our wars, and all that was lost.

Our wars have won for us every hour we live in freedom. Our wars have taken from us the men and women we honor today, and every hour of the lifetimes they had hoped to live.

This day of remembrance was first observed to recall the terrible casualties of the war Americans fought against each other. In the nearly 14 decades since, our nation's battles have all been far from home. Here on the continent of Europe were some of the fiercest of those battles, the heaviest losses, and the greatest victories.

And in all those victories American soldiers came to liberate, not to conquer. The only land we claim as our own are the resting places of our men and women.

More than 9,000 are buried here, and many times that number have — of fallen soldiers lay in our cemeteries across Europe and America. From a distance, surveying row after row of markers, we see the scale and heroism and sacrifice of the young. We think of units sustaining massive casualties, men cut down crossing a beach, or taking a hill, or securing a bridge. We think of many hundreds of sailors lost in their ships.

The war correspondent, Ernie Pyle, told of a British officer walking across the battlefield just after the violence had ended. Seeing the bodies of American boys scattered everywhere, the officer said, in sort of a hushed eulogy spoken only to himself, "Brave men, brave men."

All who come to a place like this feel the enormity of the loss. Yet, for so many, there is a marker that seems to sit alone — they come looking for that one cross, that one Star of David, that one name. Behind every grave of a fallen soldier is a story of the grief that came to a wife, a mother, a child, a family, or a town.

A World War II orphan has described her family's life after her father was killed on a field in Germany. "My mother," she said, "had lost everything she was waiting for. She lost her dreams. There were an awful lot of perfect linen tablecloths in our house that never got used, so many things being saved for a future that was never to be."

Each person buried here understood his duty, but also dreamed of going back home to the people and the things he knew. Each had plans and hopes of his own, and parted with them forever when he died.

The day will come when no one is left who knew them, when no visitor to this cemetery can stand before a grave remembering a face and a voice. The day will never come when America forgets them. And our nation and the world will always remember what they did here, and what they gave here for the future of humanity.

As dawn broke during the invasion, a little boy in the village off of Gold Beach called out to his mother, "Look, the sea is black with boats." Spread out before them and over the horizon were more than 5,000 ships and landing craft. In the skies were some of the 12,000 planes sent on the first day of Operation Overlord. The Battle of Normandy would last many days, but June 6th, 1944, was the crucial day.

The late president, Francois Mitterrand, said that nothing in history compares to D-day. "The 6th of June," he observed, "sounded the hour when history tipped toward the camp of freedom." Before dawn, the first paratroopers already had been dropped inland. The story is told of a group of French women finding Americans and imploring them not to leave. The trooper said, "We're not leaving. If necessary, this is the place we die."

Units of Army Rangers on shore, in one of history's bravest displays, scaled cliffs directly in the gunfire, never relenting even as comrades died all around them. When they had reached the top, the Rangers radioed back the code for success: "Praise the Lord."

Only a man who is there, charging out of a landing craft, can know what it was like. For the entire liberating force, there was only the ground in front of them — no shelter, no possibility of retreat. They were part of the largest amphibious landing in history, and perhaps the only great battle in which the wounded were carried forward. Survivors remember the sight of a Catholic chaplain, Father Joe Lacey, lifting dying men out of the water, and comforting and praying with them. Private Jimmy Hall was seen carrying the body of his brother, Johnny, saying, "He can't, he can't be dead. I promised Mother I'd look after him."

Such was the size of the Battle of Normandy. Thirty-eight pairs of brothers died in the liberation, including Bedford and Raymond Hoback of Virginia, both who fell on D-Day. Raymond's body was never found. All he left behind was his Bible, discovered in the sand. Their mother asked that Bedford be buried here, as well, in the place Raymond was lost, so her sons would always be together.

On Memorial Day, America honors her own. Yet we also remember all the valiant young men and women from many allied nations, including France, who shared in the struggle here, and in the suffering. We remember the men and women who served and died alongside Americans in so many terrible battles on this continent, and beyond.

Words can only go so far in capturing the grief and sense of loss for the families of those who died in all our wars. For some military families in America and in Europe, the grief is recent, with the losses we have suffered in Afghanistan. They can know, however, that the cause is just and, like other generations, these sacrifices have spared many others from tyranny and sorrow.

Long after putting away his uniform, an American GI expressed his own pride in the truth about all who served, living and dead. He said, "I feel like I played my part in turning this from a century of darkness into a century of light."

Here, where we stand today, the new world came back to liberate the old. A bond was formed of shared trial and shared victory. And a light that scattered darkness from these shores and across France would spread to all of Europe — in time, turning enemies into friends, and the pursuits of war into the pursuits of peace. Our security is still bound up together in a transatlantic alliance, with soldiers in many uniforms defending the world from terrorists at this very hour.

The grave markers here all face west, across an ageless and indifferent ocean to the country these men and women served and loved. The thoughts of America on this Memorial Day turn to them and to all their fallen comrades in arms. We think of them with lasting gratitude; we miss them with lasting love; and we pray for them. And we trust in the words of the Almighty God, which are inscribed in the chapel nearby: "I give unto them eternal life, that they shall never perish."

God bless.

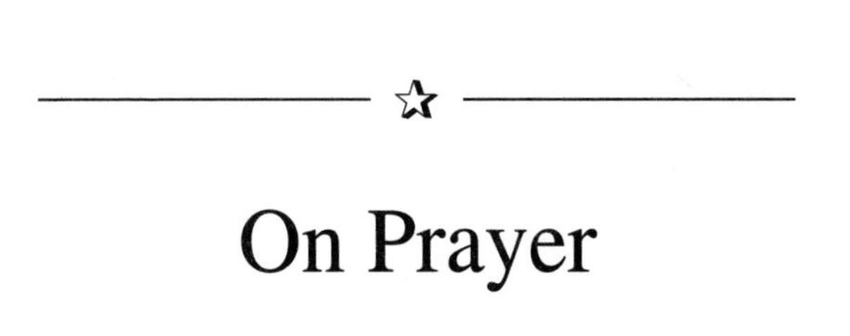

On Prayer

Prayer has served as a unifying factor in our nation.
Prayer gives us strength for the journey ahead.
–May 16, 2002

☆

We have never imposed any religion, and that's really important to remember, too. We welcome all religions in America, all religions. We honor diversity in this country. We respect people's deep convictions.

We know that men and women can be good without faith. We know that. We also know that faith is an incredibly important source of goodness in our country. Throughout our history, Americans of faith have always turned to prayer — for wisdom, prayer for resolve, prayers for compassion and strength, prayers for commitment to justice and for a spirit of forgiveness.

Since America's founding, prayer has reassured us that the hand of God is guiding the affairs of this nation. We have never asserted a special claim on His favor, yet we've always believed in God's presence in our lives. This has always been true. But it has never been more true since September the 11th.

Prayer has comforted people in grief. Prayer has served as a unifying factor in our nation. Prayer gives us strength for the journey ahead. Millions of Americans have turned to prayer during these times, and have been reminded of an important truth — while weeping may endure for a night, joy comes in the morning.

The last eight months have showed the world the American character is incredibly strong and confident. Yet prayer reminds us that a great people must be humble before God, searching for wisdom — constantly searching for wisdom — from the almighty Dios.

Prayer is a vital part of our national life. That's why your breakfast is so important. Prayer and faith are an especially vital part of the life of Hispanos in este pais. We see the role of faith in your devotion to church, to your family, and to charity. The power of faith is found among the young, and that's good news, really good news. Ministers say that a revolucion espiritual is taking place amongst los jovenes Hispanos aqui. That's good.

I want to thank you all for leading that effort. It's an important contribution to our country. One youth leader put it this way: "The revival is impacting the youth most of all, because they do not set limits on God. God is doing something so big with the youth of this nation." Those are mighty powerful words for a president to hear.

We know how important faith can be, and we know that faith without works, without action, is dead. True faith is never isolated from the rest of life.

It proves itself through actions and sacrifice, through acts of kindness and caring for those in need.

For some people, Jesus' admonition to care for "the least of these" is an admirable moral teaching. For many Hispanic Americans, it's a way of life. You understand that God has a special concern for the poor, and that community helpers and healers are doing the most important work of all — repairing broken lives, bringing love into pockets of hopelessness and despair.

Charities and community groups and faith-based institutions do incredible work in our country, really important work — providing shelters for battered women; helping the homeless; the important work of mentoring children without fathers; the work of loving a child whose mother or father may be in prison, reminding them that there is love and compassion, and decency and hope; of helping people overcome drug and alcohol addictions by helping them first and foremost change their hearts

These groups, these platoons in the armies of compassion, demonstrate compassion and inspire hope in a way that government never can. And they inspire life-changing faith in a way that government never should.

The faith-based and community initiative that I've been working on and others from Congress have been working on is really important. It's an important part of our strategy to combat hopelessness and despair and loneliness, to make America a land of opportunity and hope and promise por todos, por todos.

This set of laws will provide new incentives for

charitable giving, and that's important, really important. It will allow non-itemizers to be able to deduct a charitable gift. That will help raise money. It will help encourage the flow of people who realize it's important to not only give of their time, but of their money, as well.

When it comes to providing federal resources to effective programs, this law will make a difference, because, you see, it welcomes private and faith-based programs. It says that the days of discriminating — when it comes to the use of federal money, the days of discriminating against religious institutions simply because they are religious must come to an end.

I understand you'll be hearing from or have heard from Senator Joe Lieberman, Rick Santorum, and I know you just heard from J.C. Watts. I mention these gentlemen because first, they're fine leaders. They come from different faiths, different political parties, but are united by the common desire to pass important legislation that unleashes the strength of the country, which is the compassion of our fellow citizens. I appreciate their hard work. I appreciate their willingness to focus on the common good. I look forward to signing a bill as soon as we can get it out of the United States Senate.

You know, I often tell people that if you want to respond to what has happened to our country, you can do so with prayer, but, as importantly, you can do so by loving your neighbor like you'd like to be loved yourself. If you want to fight evil, do some good. One person cannot do everything in our society, of course. But one person can do something. And by that, I mean that we can change our country one person at a time. One person at a time. And that's what we've got to do. And that's what we have to think about.

And there's nothing more powerful in helping change the country than the faith — faith in Dios. I want to tell you, the greatest gift that people can give to a president or people in positions of responsibility — anybody else, for that matter — is prayer.

I work the ropelines a lot, and people say, "Mr. President, I pray for you and your family." I turn to them, I look them in the eye, and say, that's the greatest gift you can give. That's the greatest gift you can give. I mean it with all sincerity.

And so I want to thank you for your prayer. I want to thank you for what you do for our nation. I want to thank you for your good works. I want to thank you for helping change America one heart, one soul, one conscience at a time.

I believe that it will be said, it will be said of Americans such as yourself, "Bien, siervo bueno y fiel."

It's my honor to be with you this morning. May God bless you and your ministries, and may God continue to bless the United States of America.

On Medical Ethics

As we seek what is possible, we must always ask what is right, and we must not forget that even the most noble ends do not justify any means.
–April 10, 2002

We live in a time of tremendous medical progress. A little more than a year ago, scientists first cracked the human genetic code — one of the most important advances in scientific history. Already, scientists are developing new diagnostic tools so that each of us can know our risk of disease and act to prevent them.

One day soon, precise therapies will be custom made for our own genetic makeup. We're on the threshold of historic breakthroughs against AIDS and Alzheimer's Disease and cancer and diabetes and heart disease and Parkinson's Disease. And that's incredibly positive.

Our age may be known to history as the age of genetic medicine, a time when many of the most feared illnesses were overcome.

Our age must also be defined by the care and restraint and responsibility with which we take up these new scientific powers.

Advances in biomedical technology must never come at the expense of human conscience. As we seek what is possible, we must always ask what is right, and we must not forget that even the most noble ends do not justify any means.

Science has set before us decisions of immense consequence. We can pursue medical research with a clear sense of moral purpose or we can travel without an ethical compass into a world we could live to regret. Science now presses forward the issue of human cloning. How we answer the question of human cloning will place us on one path or the other.

Human cloning is the laboratory production of individuals who are genetically identical to another human being. Cloning is achieved by putting the genetic material from a donor into a woman's egg, which has had its nucleus removed. As a result, the new or cloned embryo is an identical copy of only the donor. Human cloning has moved from science fiction into science.

One biotech company has already began producing embryonic human clones for research purposes. Chinese scientists have derived stem cells from cloned embryos created by combining human DNA and rabbit eggs. Others have announced plans to produce cloned children, despite the fact that laboratory cloning of animals has lead to spontaneous abortions and terrible, terrible abnormalities.

Human cloning is deeply troubling to me, and to most Americans. Life is a creation, not a commodity. Our children are gifts to be loved and protected, not products to be designed and manufactured.

Allowing cloning would be taking a significant step toward a society in which human beings are grown for spare body parts, and children are engineered to custom specifications; and that's not acceptable.

In the current debate over human cloning, two terms are being used: reproductive cloning and research cloning. Reproductive cloning involves creating a cloned embryo and implanting it into a woman with the goal of creating a child. Fortunately, nearly every American agrees that this practice should be banned. Research cloning, on the other hand, involves the creation of cloned human embryos which are then destroyed to derive stem cells.

I believe all human cloning is wrong, and both forms of cloning ought to be banned, for the following reasons. First, anything other than a total ban on human cloning would be unethical. Research cloning would contradict the most fundamental principle of medical ethics, that no human life should be exploited or extinguished for the benefit of another.

Yet a law permitting research cloning, while forbidding the birth of a cloned child, would require the destruction of nascent human life. Secondly, anything other than a total ban on human cloning would be virtually impossible to enforce. Cloned human embryos created for research would be widely available in laboratories and embryo farms. Once cloned embryos were available, implantation would take place. Even the tightest regulations and strict policing would not prevent or detect the birth of cloned babies.

Third, the benefits of research cloning are highly

speculative. Advocates of research cloning argue that stem cells obtained from cloned embryos would be injected into a genetically identical individual without risk of tissue rejection. But there is evidence, based on animal studies, that cells derived from cloned embryos may indeed be rejected.

Yet even if research cloning were medically effective, every person who wanted to benefit would need an embryonic clone of his or her own, to provide the designer tissues. This would create a massive national market for eggs and egg donors, and exploitation of women's bodies that we cannot and must not allow.

I stand firm in my opposition to human cloning. And at the same time, we will pursue other promising and ethical ways to relieve suffering through biotechnology. This year for the first time, federal dollars will go towards supporting human embryonic stem cell research consistent with the ethical guidelines I announced last August.

The National Institutes of Health is also funding a broad range of animal and human adult stem cell research. Adult stem cells which do not require the destruction of human embryos and which yield tissues which can be transplanted without rejection are more versatile that originally thought.

We're making progress. We're learning more about them. And therapies developed from adult stem cells are already helping suffering people.

I support increasing the research budget of the NIH, and I ask Congress to join me in that support. And at the same time, I strongly support a comprehensive law against all human cloning. And I endorse the bill — wholeheartedly endorse the bill — sponsored by Senator Brownback and Senator Mary Landrieu.

This carefully drafted bill would ban all human cloning in the United States, including the cloning of embryos for research. It is nearly identical to the bipartisan legislation that last year passed the House of Representatives by more than a 100-vote margin. It has wide support across the political spectrum, liberals and conservatives support it, religious people and nonreligious people support it. Those who are pro-choice and those who are pro-life support the bill.

This is a diverse coalition, united by a commitment to prevent the cloning and exploitation of human beings. It would be a mistake for the United States Senate to allow any kind of human cloning to come out of that chamber.

I'm an incurable optimist about the future of our country. I know we can achieve great things. We can make the world more peaceful, we can become a more compassionate nation. We can push the limits of medical science. I truly believe that we're going to bring hope and healing to countless lives across the country. And as we do, I will insist that we always maintain the highest of ethical standards.

Thank you all for coming. God bless.

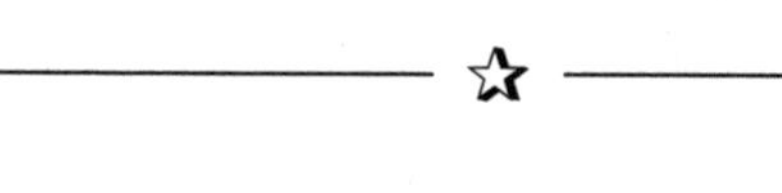

On Resolve

This nation is peaceful, but fierce when stirred to anger. This conflict was begun on the timing and terms of others. It will end in a way, and at an hour, of our choosing.
–SEPTEMBER 14, 2001

We are here in the middle hour of our grief. So many have suffered so great a loss, and today we express our nation's sorrow. We come before God to pray for the missing and the dead, and for those who love them.

On Tuesday, our country was attacked with deliberate and massive cruelty. We have seen the images of fire and ashes, and bent steel.

Now come the names, the list of casualties we are only beginning to read. They are the names of men and women who began their day at a desk or in an airport, busy with life. They are the names of people who faced death, and in their last moments called home to say, be brave, and I love you.

They are the names of passengers who defied their murderers, and prevented the murder of others on the ground. They are the names of men and women who wore the uniform of the United States, and died at their posts.

They are the names of rescuers, the ones whom death found running up the stairs and into the fires to help others. We will read all these names. We will linger over them, and learn their stories, and many Americans will weep.

To the children and parents and spouses and families and friends of the lost, we offer the deepest sympathy of the nation. And I assure you, you are not alone.

Just three days removed from these events, Americans do not yet have the distance of history. But our responsibility to history is already clear: to answer these attacks and rid the world of evil.

War has been waged against us by stealth and deceit and murder. This nation is peaceful, but fierce when stirred to anger. This conflict was begun on the timing and terms of others. It will end in a way, and at an hour, of our choosing.

Our purpose as a nation is firm. Yet our wounds as a people are recent and unhealed, and lead us to pray. In many of our prayers this week, there is a searching, and an honesty. At St. Patrick's Cathedral in New York on Tuesday, a woman said, "I prayed to God to give us a sign that He is still here." Others have prayed for the same, searching hospital to hospital, carrying pictures of those still missing.

God's signs are not always the ones we look for. We learn in tragedy that His purposes are not always our own. Yet the prayers of private suffering, whether in our homes or in this great cathedral, are known and heard, and understood.

There are prayers that help us last through the day, or endure the night. There are prayers of friends and strangers that give us strength for the journey. And there are prayers that yield our will to a will greater than our own.

This world He created is of moral design. Grief and tragedy and hatred are only for a time. Goodness, remembrance, and love have no end. And the Lord of life holds all who die, and all who mourn.

It is said that adversity introduces us to ourselves. This is true of a nation as well. In this trial, we have been reminded, and the world has seen, that our fellow Americans are generous and kind, resourceful and brave. We see our national character in rescuers working past exhaustion; in long lines of blood donors; in thousands of citizens who have asked to work and serve in any way possible.

And we have seen our national character in eloquent acts of sacrifice. Inside the World Trade Center, one man who could have saved himself stayed until the end at the side of his quadriplegic friend. A beloved priest died giving the last rites to a firefighter. Two office workers, finding a disabled stranger, carried her down sixty-eight floors to safety. A group of men drove through the night from Dallas to Washington to bring skin grafts for burn victims.

In these acts, and in many others, Americans showed a deep commitment to one another, and an abiding love for our country. Today, we feel what Franklin Roosevelt called the warm courage of national unity. This is a unity of every faith, and every background.

It has joined together political parties in both houses of Congress. It is evident in services of prayer and candlelight vigils, and American flags, which are displayed in pride, and wave in defiance.

Our unity is a kinship of grief, and a steadfast resolve to prevail against our enemies. And this unity against terror is now extending across the world.

America is a nation full of good fortune, with so much to be grateful for. But we are not spared from suffering. In every generation, the world has produced enemies of human freedom. They have attacked America, because we are freedom's home and defender. And the commitment of our fathers is now the calling of our time.

On this national day of prayer and remembrance, we ask almighty God to watch over our nation, and grant us patience and resolve in all that is to come. We pray that He will comfort and console those who now walk in sorrow. We thank Him for each life we now must mourn, and the promise of a life to come.

As we have been assured, neither death nor life, nor angels nor principalities nor powers, nor things present nor things to come, nor height nor depth, can separate us from God's love. May He bless the souls of the departed. May He comfort our own. And may He always guide our country.

God bless America.

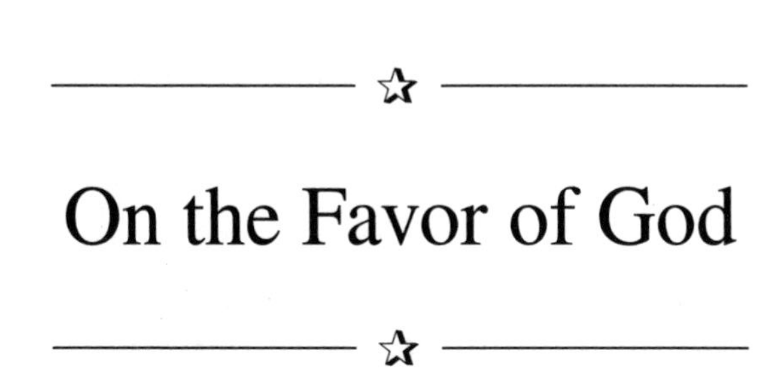

On the Favor of God

We cannot presume to know every design of our Creator,
or to assert a special claim on His favor.
Yet, it is important to pause and recognize our help
in ages past and our hope for years to come.
–MAY 3, 2001

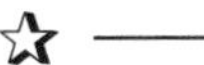

This is a day when our nation recognizes a power above our power, and influence beyond our influence, a guiding wisdom far greater than our own. The American character, it's strong and confident; but we have never been reluctant to speak of our own dependence on providence.

Our country was founded by great and wise people who were fluent in the language of humility, praise and petition. Throughout our history, in danger and division, we have always turned to prayer. And our country has been delivered from many serious evils and wrongs because of that prayer.

We cannot presume to know every design of our Creator, or to assert a special claim on His favor. Yet, it is important to pause and recognize our help in ages past and our hope for years to come.

The first president to live in the White House

arrived with a prayer. In a letter to his wife, written on his second night here, John Adams offered a prayer that Heaven might bless this house and all those who would call it home. One of his successors, Franklin D. Roosevelt, thought enough of that prayer to have it inscribed on a mantlepiece in the State Dining Room, where you can still find it today.

In this house, I make many decisions. But as I do so, as I make those decisions, I know as surely as you said that many Americans lift me up in prayer. Those prayers are a gracious gift, and Laura and I and my family greatly appreciate them.

America has many traditions of faith and many experiences of prayer. But I suspect that many who pray have something in common: that we may pray for God's help, but as we do so, we find that God has changed our deepest selves. We learn humility before His will and acceptance of things beyond our understanding. We discover that the most sincere of all prayers can be the simple words, "Thy will be done." And that is a comfort more powerful than all our plans.

Laura and I really appreciate you being here on this special day. We thank you for your concerns for your country and your love of the Lord. It's an honor for me to be here and I would ask that you join me in the State Dining Room for a little fellowship.

God bless America.

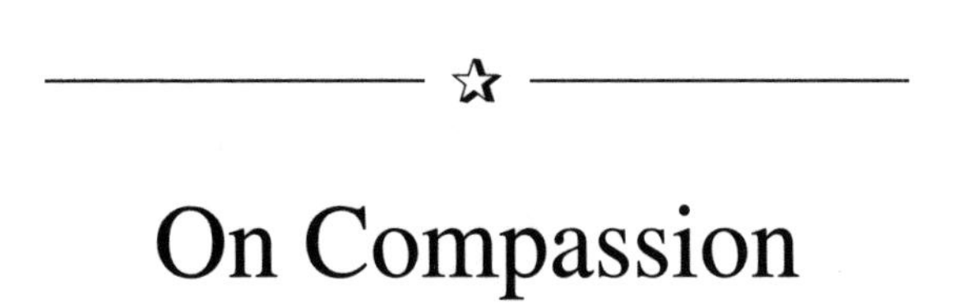

On Compassion

Government cannot solve every problem, but it can encourage people and communities to help themselves and to help one another.
–April 30, 2002

☆

Every American must believe in the promise of America. And to reach this noble, necessary goal, there is a role for government. America doesn't need more big government, and we've learned that more money is not always the answer. If a program is failing to serve people, it makes little difference if we spend twice as much or half as much. The measure of true compassion is results.

Yet we cannot have an indifferent government either. We are a generous and caring people. We don't believe in a sink-or-swim society. The policies of our government must heed the universal call of all faiths to love a neighbor as we would want to be loved ourselves. We need a different approach than either big government or indifferent government. We need a government that is focused, effective, and close to the people; a government that does a few things, and does them well.

Government cannot solve every problem, but it

can encourage people and communities to help themselves and to help one another. Often the truest kind of compassion is to help citizens build lives of their own. I call my philosophy and approach "compassionate conservatism." It is compassionate to actively help our fellow citizens in need. It is conservative to insist on responsibility and on results. And with this hopeful approach, we can make a real difference in people's lives.

Compassionate conservatism places great hope and confidence in public education. Our economy depends on higher and higher skills, requiring every American to have the basic tools of learning. Every public school should be the path of upward mobility.

Yet, sadly enough, many are the dead-end of dreams. Public schools are some of the most important institutions of democracy. They take children of every background, from every part of the world, and prepare them for the obligations and opportunities of a free society. Public schools are America's great hope, and making them work for every child is America's great duty.

The new education reforms we have passed in Washington give the federal government a new role in public education. Schools must meet new and high standards of performance in reading and math that will be proven on tests and posted on the Internet for parents and everyone to see. And we're giving local schools and teachers unprecedented freedom and resources and training to meet these goals.

It is conservative to let local communities chart their own path to excellence. It is compassionate to insist that every child learns, so that no child is left behind. By insisting on results, and challenging failure where we find it, we'll make an incredible difference in the lives of every child in America.

Compassionate conservatism offers a new vision for fighting poverty in America. For decades, our nation has devoted enormous resources to helping the poor, with some great successes to show for it: basic medical care for those in need, a better life for elderly Americans. However, for millions of younger Americans, welfare became a static and destructive way of life.

In 1996, we began transforming welfare with time limits and job training and work requirements. And the nation's welfare rolls have been cut by more than half. But even more importantly, many lives have been dramatically improved.

One former welfare recipient here in California, who happened to be a mother of a chronically ill child and the victim of domestic violence, describes her experience upon leaving welfare. She said, "I feel like an adult again. I have my dignity back."

We need to continue to fully transform welfare in America. As Congress takes up welfare reform again in the coming weeks, we must strengthen the work requirements that prevent dependency and despair. Millions of Americans once on welfare are finding that a job is more than a source of income. It is a source of dignity. And by helping people find work, by helping them prepare for work, we practice compassion.

Welfare reform must also, wherever possible,

encourage the commitments of family. Not every child has two devoted parents at home — I understand that. And not every marriage can, or should be saved. But the evidence shows that strong marriages are good for children.

When a couple on welfare wants to break bad patterns and start or strengthen a marriage, we should help local groups give them counseling that teaches commitment and respect. By encouraging family, we practice compassion.

In overcoming poverty and dependence, we must also promote the work of charities and community groups and faith-based institutions. These organizations, such as shelters for battered women or mentoring programs for fatherless children or drug treatment centers, inspire hope in a way that government never can. Often, they inspire life-changing faith in a way that government never should.

Our government should view the good Americans that work in faith-based charities as partners, not rivals. We must provide new incentives for charitable giving and, when it comes to providing federal resources to effective programs, we should not discriminate against private and religious groups.

I urge the Senate to pass the faith-based initiative for the good of America. It is compassionate to aggressively fight poverty in America. It is conservative to encourage work and community spirit and responsibility and the values that often come from faith. And with this approach, we can change lives one soul at a time, and make a real difference in the lives of our citizens.

The same principles of compassion and responsibility apply when America offers assistance to other nations. Nearly half of the world's people still live on less than $2 a day. When we help them, we show our values, our belief in universal human dignity. We serve our interests and gain economic partners. And by helping the developing nations of the world, we offer an alternative to resentment and conflict and terror.

Yet the old way of pouring vast amounts of money into development aid without any concern for results has failed, often leaving behind misery and poverty and corruption. America's offering a new compact for global development. Greater aid contributions from America must be and will be linked to greater responsibility from developing nations.

I have proposed a 50-percent increase in our core development assistance over the next three budget years, money that will be placed in a new Millennium Challenge Account. At the end of this three-year period, the level of our annual development assistance will be $5 billion higher than current levels.

This is a record amount of spending. And in return for these funds, we expect nations to rout out corruption, to open their markets, to respect human rights, and to adhere to the rule of law. And these are the keys to progress in any nation, and they will be the conditions for any new American aid.

It is compassionate to increase our international aid. It is conservative to require the hard reforms that lead to prosperity and independence. And with this approach, we'll make a real difference in the lives of people around the world.

Compassionate conservatism guides my administration in many other areas. Our health care policies must help low-income Americans to buy health insurance they choose, they own and they control. Our environmental policy set high standards for stewardship, while allowing local cooperation and innovation to meet those standards. Our housing programs moved beyond rental assistance to the pride and stability of home ownership. Our reforms in Social Security must allow and encourage and help working Americans to build up their own asset base and achieve independence for their retirement years.

All of these policies and all of these areas serve the same vision. We are using an active government to promote self-government. We're encouraging individuals and communities and families to take more and more responsibility for themselves, for their neighbors, for our nation. The aim of these policies is not to spend more money or spend less money; it is to spend on what works.

The measure of compassion is more than good intentions; it is good results. Sympathy is not enough. We need solutions in America, and we know where solutions are found. When schools are teaching, when families are strong, when neighbors look after their neighbors, when our people have the tools and the skills and the resources they need to improve their lives, there is no problem that cannot be solved in America.

By being involved and by taking responsibility upon ourselves, we gain something else, as well: We contribute to the life of our country. We become more than taxpayers and occasional voters; we become citizens. Citizens, not spectators. Citizens who hear the call of duty, who stand up for their beliefs, who care for their families, who control their lives, and who treat their neighbors with respect and compassion. We discover a satisfaction that is only found in service, and we show our gratitude to America and to those who came before us.

In the last seven months, we've been tested, and the struggle of our time has revealed the spirit of our people. Since September the 11th, we have been the kind of nation our founders had in mind: a nation of strong and confident and self-governing people. And we've been the kind of nation our fathers and mothers defended in World War II: a great and diverse country, united by common dangers and by common resolve.

We in our time will defend our nation, and we will deliver our nation's promise to all who seek it. In our war on terror, we are showing the world the strength of our country, and by our unity and tolerance and compassion, we will show the world the soul of our country. May God bless America.

On Religious Freedom

Today, as America wages war against terror, our resolve to defend religious freedom remains as strong as ever.
–JANUARY 16, 2002

Religious freedom is a cornerstone of our Republic, a core principle of our Constitution, and a fundamental human right. Many of those who first settled in America, such as Pilgrims, came for the freedom of worship and belief that this new land promised. And when the British Colonies became the United States, our Founders constitutionally limited our Federal Government's capacity to interfere with religious belief by prohibiting the Congress from passing any law "respecting an establishment of religion, or prohibiting the free exercise thereof." These constitutional limits have allowed the flourishing of faith across our country, which greatly blesses our land.

George Washington forcefully expressed our collective constitutional promise to protect the rights of people of all faiths, in a historic letter he wrote to the Jewish community at Touro Synagogue in Newport, Rhode Island: "the Government of the United States, which gives to bigotry no sanction, to persecution no assistance, requires only that they who live under its protection should demean themselves as good citizens...." Today, our cities are home to synagogues, churches, temples, mosques, and other houses of worship that peacefully welcome Americans of every belief. Preserving religious freedom has helped America avoid the wars of religion that have plagued so many cultures throughout history, with deadly consequences.

Today, as America wages war against terror, our resolve to defend religious freedom remains as strong as ever. Many miles from home, American service men and women have risked their lives in our efforts to drive the Taliban regime from power, ending an era of brutal oppression, including religious oppression. At home, Americans demonstrated the vitality of our religious freedom in the enormous outreach by faith communities to help those harmed by the terrorist attacks. In quiet prayers offered to God in churches, synagogues, temples, and mosques and in the helping hands of faith-based groups, Americans have shown a deep love for others and genuine spiritual unity that will sustain us through the difficult days of recovery.

Religious Freedom Day provides us an opportunity to celebrate America's commitment to protect the freedom of religion. On this special day, I encourage all Americans to renew their commitment to protecting the liberties that make our country a beacon of hope for people around the world who seek the free exercise of religious beliefs and other freedoms.

☆

On Protecting Unborn Children

☆

We are a society with enough compassion and wealth and love to care for both mothers and their children, and to seek the promise and potential of every single life.
–JANUARY 22, 2002

☆

For almost 30 years, Americans from every state in the Union have gathered in the Washington Mall in order to march for life. This march is an example of an inspiring commitment and of deep human compassion.

Everyone there believes, as I do, that every life is valuable; that our society has a responsibility to defend the vulnerable and weak, the imperfect and even the unwanted; and that our nation should set a great goal that unborn children should be welcomed in life and protected in law.

Abortion is an issue that deeply divides our country. And we need to treat those with whom we disagree with respect and civility. We must overcome bitterness and rancor where we find it and seek common ground where we can. But we will continue to speak out on behalf of the most vulnerable members of our society.

We do so because we believe the promises of the

Declaration of Independence are the common code of American life. They should apply to everyone, not just the healthy or the strong or the powerful. A generous society values all human life. A merciful society seeks to expand legal protection to every life, including early life. And a compassionate society will defend a simple, moral proposition: Life should never be used as a tool, or a means to an end.

These are bedrock principles and that is why my administration opposes partial-birth abortion and public funding for abortion; why we support teen abstinence and crisis pregnancy programs, adoption and parental notification laws; and why we are against all forms of human cloning.

And that is why I urge the United States Senate to support a comprehensive and effective ban on human cloning, a ban that was passed by an overwhelming and bipartisan vote of the House of Representatives last July

We are a society with enough compassion and wealth and love to care for both mothers and their children, and to seek the promise and potential of every single life. You're working and marching on behalf of a noble cause, and affirming a culture of life. Thank you for your persistence, for defending human dignity, and for caring for every member of the human family.

May God continue to bless America. Thank you very much.

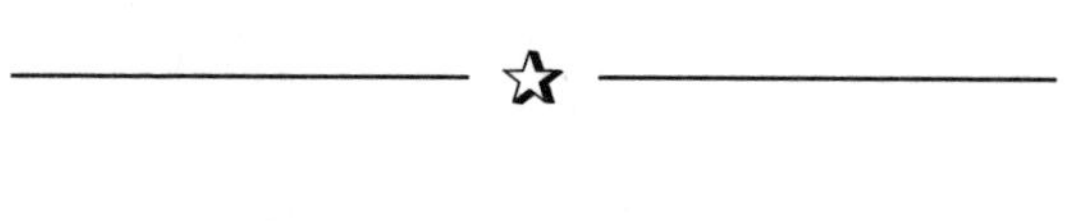

On Freedom

By definition, the success of freedom rests upon the choices and the courage of free peoples, and upon their willingness to sacrifice.
–November 6, 2003

The roots of our democracy can be traced to England, and to its Parliament — and so can the roots of this organization. In June of 1982, President Ronald Reagan spoke at Westminster Palace and declared, the turning point had arrived in history. He argued that Soviet communism had failed, precisely because it did not respect its own people — their creativity, their genius and their rights.

President Reagan said that the day of Soviet tyranny was passing, that freedom had a momentum which would not be halted. He gave this organization its mandate: to add to the momentum of freedom across the world. Your mandate was important 20 years ago; it is equally important today.

A number of critics were dismissive of that speech by the president. According to one editorial of the time, "It seems hard to be a sophisticated European and also an admirer of Ronald Reagan." Some observers on both sides of the Atlantic pronounced the speech simplistic and naive, and even dangerous. In fact, Ronald Reagan's words were courageous and optimistic and entirely correct.

The great democratic movement President Reagan described was already well underway. In the early 1970s, there were about 40 democracies in the world. By the middle of that decade, Portugal and Spain and Greece held free elections. Soon there were new democracies in Latin America, and free institutions were spreading in Korea, in Taiwan, and in East Asia. This very week in 1989, there were protests in East Berlin and in Leipzig. By the end of that year, every communist dictatorship in Central America had collapsed. Within another year, the South African government released Nelson Mandela. Four years later, he was elected president of his country — ascending, like Walesa and Havel, from prisoner of state to head of state.

As the 20th century ended, there were around 120 democracies in the world — and I can assure you more are on the way. Ronald Reagan would be pleased, and he would not be surprised.

We've witnessed, in little over a generation, the swiftest advance of freedom in the 2,500-year story of democracy. Historians in the future will offer their own explanations for why this happened. Yet we already know some of the reasons they will cite. It is no accident that the rise of so many democracies took place in a time when the world's most influential nation was itself a democracy.

The United States made military and moral commitments in Europe and Asia, which protected free nations from aggression and created the conditions in which new democracies could flourish. As we provided security for whole nations, we also provided inspiration for oppressed peoples. In prison camps, in banned union meetings, in clandestine churches, men and women knew that the whole world was not sharing their own nightmare. They knew of at least one place — a bright and hopeful land — where freedom was valued and secure. And they prayed that America would not forget them, or forget the mission to promote liberty around the world.

Historians will note that in many nations, the advance of markets and free enterprise helped to create a middle class that was confident enough to demand their own rights. They will point to the role of technology in frustrating censorship and central control — and marvel at the power of instant communications to spread the truth, the news, and courage across borders.

Historians in the future will reflect on an extraordinary, undeniable fact: Over time, free nations grow stronger and dictatorships grow weaker. In the middle of the 20th century, some imagined that the central planning and social regimentation were a shortcut to national strength. In fact, the prosperity and social vitality and technological progress of a people are directly determined by extent of their liberty. Freedom honors and unleashes human creativity — and creativity determines the strength and wealth of nations. Liberty is both the plan of Heaven for humanity, and the best hope for progress here on Earth.

The progress of liberty is a powerful trend. Yet, we also know that liberty, if not defended, can be lost. The success of freedom is not determined by some dialectic of history. By definition, the success of freedom rests upon the choices and the courage of free peoples, and upon their willingness to sacrifice. In the trenches of World War I, through a two-front war in the 1940s, the difficult battles of Korea and Vietnam, and in missions of rescue and liberation on nearly every continent, Americans have amply displayed our willingness to sacrifice for liberty.

The sacrifices of Americans have not always been recognized or appreciated, yet they have been worthwhile. Because we and our allies were steadfast, Germany and Japan are democratic nations that no longer threaten the world. A global nuclear standoff with the Soviet Union ended peacefully — as did the Soviet Union. The nations of Europe are moving towards unity, not dividing into armed camps and descending into genocide. Every nation has learned, or should have learned, an important lesson: Freedom is worth fighting for, dying for, and standing for — and the advance of freedom leads to peace.

And now we must apply that lesson in our own time. We've reached another great turning point — and the resolve we show will shape the next stage of the world democratic movement.

Our commitment to democracy is tested in countries like Cuba and Burma and North Korea and Zimbabwe — outposts of oppression in our world. The people in these nations live in captivity and fear and silence. Yet, these regimes cannot hold back freedom forever — and, one day, from prison camps and prison cells and from exile, the leaders of new democracies will arrive. Communism and militarism and rule by the capricious and corrupt are the relics of a passing era. And we will stand with these oppressed peoples until the day of their freedom finally arrives.

Our commitment to democracy is tested in China. That nation now has a sliver, a fragment of liberty. Yet, China's people will eventually want their liberty pure and whole. China has discovered that economic freedom leads to national wealth. China's leaders will also discover that freedom is indivisible — that social and religious freedom is also essential to national greatness and national dignity. Eventually, men and women who are allowed to control their own wealth will insist on controlling their own lives and their own country.

Our commitment to democracy is also tested in the Middle East, which is my focus today, and must be a focus of American policy for decades to come. In many nations of the Middle East — countries of great strategic importance — democracy has not yet taken root. And the questions arise: Are the peoples of the Middle East somehow beyond the reach of liberty? Are millions of men and women and children condemned by history or culture to live in despotism? Are they alone never to know freedom, and never even to have a choice in the matter? I, for one, do not believe it. I believe every person has the ability and the right to be free.

Some skeptics of democracy assert that the traditions of Islam are inhospitable to the representative government. This "cultural condescension," as Ronald Reagan termed it, has a long history. After the Japanese surrender in 1945, a so-called Japan expert asserted that democracy in that former empire would "never work." Another observer declared the prospects for democracy in post-Hitler Germany are, and I quote, "most uncertain at best" — he made that claim in 1957. Seventy-four years ago, The Sunday *London Times* declared nine-tenths of the population of India to be "illiterates not caring a fig for politics." Yet when Indian democracy was imperiled in the 1970s, the Indian people showed their commitment to liberty in a national referendum that saved their form of government.

Time after time, observers have questioned whether this country, or that people, or this group, are "ready" for democracy — as if freedom were a prize you win for meeting our own Western standards of progress. In fact, the daily work of democracy itself is the path of progress. It teaches cooperation, the free exchange of ideas, and the peaceful resolution of differences. As men and women are showing, from Bangladesh to Botswana to Mongolia, it is the practice of democracy that makes a nation ready for democracy, and every nation can start on this path.

It should be clear to all that Islam — the faith of one-fifth of humanity — is consistent with democratic rule. Democratic progress is found in many predominantly Muslim countries — in Turkey and Indonesia, and Senegal and Albania, Niger and Sierra Leone. Muslim men and women are good citizens of India and South Africa, of the nations of Western Europe, and of the United States of America.

More than half of all the Muslims in the world live in freedom under democratically constituted governments. They succeed in democratic societies, not in spite of their faith, but because of it. A religion that demands individual moral accountability, and encourages the encounter of the individual with God, is fully compatible with the rights and responsibilities of self-government.

Yet there's a great challenge today in the Middle East. In the words of a recent report by Arab scholars, the global wave of democracy has — and I quote — "barely reached the Arab states." They continue: "This freedom deficit undermines human development and is one of the most painful manifestations of lagging political development." The freedom deficit they describe has terrible consequences, of the people of the Middle East and for the world. In many Middle Eastern countries, poverty is deep and it is spreading, women lack rights and are denied schooling. Whole societies remain stagnant while the world moves ahead. These are not the failures of a culture or a religion. These are the failures of political and economic doctrines.

As the colonial era passed away, the Middle East saw the establishment of many military dictatorships. Some rulers adopted the dogmas of socialism, seized total control of political parties and the media and universities. They allied themselves with the Soviet bloc and with international terrorism. Dictators in Iraq and Syria promised the restoration of national honor, a return to ancient glories. They've left instead a legacy of torture, oppression, misery, and ruin.

Other men, and groups of men, have gained influence in the Middle East and beyond through an ideology of theocratic terror. Behind their language of religion is the ambition for absolute political power. Ruling cabals like the Taliban show their version of religious piety in public whippings of women, ruthless suppression of any difference or dissent, and support for terrorists who arm and train to murder the innocent. The Taliban promised religious purity and national pride. Instead, by systematically destroying a proud and working society, they left behind suffering and starvation.

Many Middle Eastern governments now understand that military dictatorship and theocratic rule are a straight, smooth highway to nowhere. But some governments still cling to the old habits of central control. There are governments that still fear and repress independent thought and creativity, and private enterprise — the human qualities that make for a strong and successful societies. Even when these nations have vast natural resources, they do not respect or develop their greatest resources — the talent and energy of men and women working and living in freedom.

Instead of dwelling on past wrongs and blaming others, governments in the Middle East need to confront real problems, and serve the true interests of their nations. The good and capable people of the Middle East all deserve responsible leadership. For too long, many people in that region have been victims and subjects — they deserve to be active citizens.

Governments across the Middle East and North Africa are beginning to see the need for change. Morocco has a diverse new parliament; King

Mohammed has urged it to extend the rights to women. Here is how His Majesty explained his reforms to parliament: "How can society achieve progress while women, who represent half the nation, see their rights violated and suffer as a result of injustice, violence, and marginalization, notwithstanding the dignity and justice granted to them by our glorious religion?" The King of Morocco is correct: The future of Muslim nations will be better for all with the full participation of women.

In Bahrain last year, citizens elected their own parliament for the first time in nearly three decades. Oman has extended the vote to all adult citizens; Qatar has a new constitution; Yemen has a multiparty political system; Kuwait has a directly elected national assembly; and Jordan held historic elections this summer. Recent surveys in Arab nations reveal broad support for political pluralism, the rule of law, and free speech. These are the stirrings of Middle Eastern democracy, and they carry the promise of greater change to come.

As changes come to the Middle Eastern region, those with power should ask themselves: Will they be remembered for resisting reform, or for leading it? In Iran, the demand for democracy is strong and broad, as we saw last month when thousands gathered to welcome home Shirin Ebadi, the winner of the Nobel Peace Prize. The regime in Teheran must heed the democratic demands of the Iranian people, or lose its last claim to legitimacy.

For the Palestinian people, the only path to independence and dignity and progress is the path of democracy. And the Palestinian leaders who block and undermine democratic reform, and feed hatred and encourage violence, are not leaders at all. They're the main obstacles to peace, and to the success of the Palestinian people.

The Saudi government is taking first steps toward reform, including a plan for gradual introduction of elections. By giving the Saudi people a greater role in their own society, the Saudi government can demonstrate true leadership in the region.

The great and proud nation of Egypt has shown the way toward peace in the Middle East, and now should show the way toward democracy in the Middle East. Champions of democracy in the region understand that democracy is not perfect, it is not the path to utopia, but it's the only path to national success and dignity.

As we watch and encourage reforms in the region, we are mindful that modernization is not the same as Westernization. Representative governments in the Middle East will reflect their own cultures. They will not, and should not, look like us. Democratic nations may be constitutional monarchies, federal republics, or parliamentary systems. And working democracies always need time to develop — as did our own. We've taken a 200-year journey toward inclusion and justice — and this makes us patient and understanding as other nations are at different stages of this journey.

There are, however, essential principles common to every successful society, in every culture. Successful societies limit the power of the state and the power of the military — so that governments respond to the will of the people, and not the will of an elite. Successful societies protect freedom with the consistent and impartial rule of law, instead of selecting applying — selectively applying the law to punish political opponents. Successful societies allow room for healthy civic institutions — for political parties and labor unions and independent newspapers and broadcast media. Successful societies guarantee religious liberty — the right to serve and honor God without fear of persecution. Successful societies privatize their economies, and secure the rights of property. They prohibit and punish official corruption, and invest in the health and education of their people. They recognize the rights of women. And instead of directing hatred and resentment against others, successful societies appeal to the hopes of their own people.

These vital principles are being applied in the nations of Afghanistan and Iraq. With the steady leadership of President Karzai, the people of Afghanistan are building a modern and peaceful government. Next month, 500 delegates will convene a national assembly in Kabul to approve a new Afghan constitution. The proposed draft would establish a bicameral parliament, set national elections next year, and recognize Afghanistan's Muslim identity, while protecting the rights of all citizens. Afghanistan faces continuing economic and security challenges — it will face those challenges as a free and stable democracy.

In Iraq, the Coalition Provisional Authority and the Iraqi Governing Council are also working together to build a democracy — and after three decades of tyranny, this work is not easy. The former dictator ruled by terror and treachery, and left deeply ingrained habits of fear and distrust. Remnants of his regime, joined by foreign terrorists, continue their battle against order and against civilization. Our coalition is responding to recent attacks with precision raids, guided by intelligence provided by the Iraqis themselves. And we're working closely with Iraqi citizens as they prepare a constitution, as they move toward free elections and take increasing responsibility for their own affairs. As in the defense of Greece in 1947, and later in the Berlin Airlift, the strength and will of free peoples are now being tested before a watching world. And we will meet this test.

Securing democracy in Iraq is the work of many hands. American and coalition forces are sacrificing for the peace of Iraq and for the security of free nations. Aid workers from many countries are facing danger to help the Iraqi people. The National Endowment for Democracy is promoting women's rights, and training Iraqi journalists, and teaching the skills of political participation. Iraqis, themselves — police and borders guards and local officials — are joining in the work and they are sharing in the sacrifice.

This is a massive and difficult undertaking — it is worth our effort, it is worth our sacrifice, because we know the stakes. The failure of Iraqi democracy would embolden terrorists around the world, increase dangers to the American people, and extinguish the hopes of millions in the region. Iraqi democracy will succeed — and that success will send forth the news, from Damascus to Teheran — that freedom can be the future of every nation. The establishment of a free Iraq at the heart of the Middle East will be a watershed event in the global democratic revolution

Sixty years of Western nations excusing and accommodating the lack of freedom in the Middle East did nothing to make us safe — because in the long run, stability cannot be purchased at the expense of liberty. As long as the Middle East remains a place where freedom does not flourish, it will remain a place of stagnation, resentment, and violence ready for export. And with the spread of weapons that can bring catastrophic harm to our country and to our friends, it would be reckless to accept the status quo.

Therefore, the United States has adopted a new policy, a forward strategy of freedom in the Middle East. This strategy requires the same persistence and energy and idealism we have shown before. And it will yield the same results. As in Europe, as in Asia, as in every region of the world, the advance of freedom leads to peace.

The advance of freedom is the calling of our time; it is the calling of our country. From the Fourteen Points to the Four Freedoms, to the Speech at Westminster, America has put our power at the service of principle. We believe that liberty is the design of nature; we believe that liberty is the direction of history. We believe that human fulfillment and excellence come in the responsible exercise of liberty. And we believe that freedom — the freedom we prize — is not for us alone; it is the right and the capacity of all mankind.

Working for the spread of freedom can be hard.

Yet, America has accomplished hard tasks before. Our nation is strong; we're strong of heart. And we're not alone. Freedom is finding allies in every country; freedom finds allies in every culture. And as we meet the terror and violence of the world, we can be certain the author of freedom is not indifferent to the fate of freedom.

With all the tests and all the challenges of our age, this is, above all, the age of liberty. Each of you at this Endowment is fully engaged in the great cause of liberty. And I thank you. May God bless your work. And may God continue to bless America.

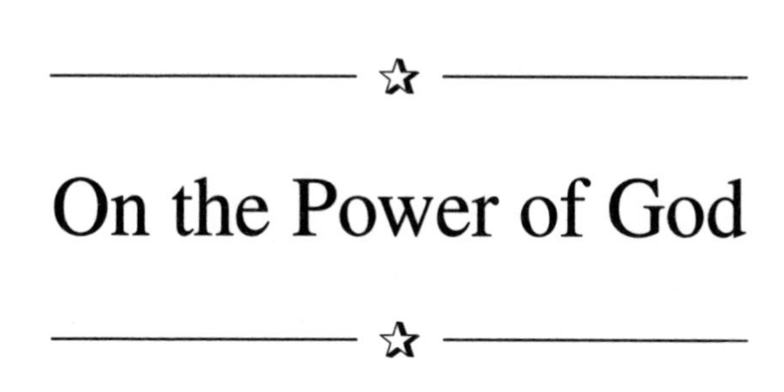

On the Power of God

His is not the power of armies or technology or wealth.
It is the unexpected power of a baby in a stable,
of a man on a cross, of a simple fisherman who
carried a message of hope to Rome.
–MARCH 22, 2001

When Cardinal Wojtyla spoke here at Catholic University in 1976, few imagined the course his life would take, or the history his life would shape. In 1978, most of the world knew him only as the Polish Pope. There were signs of something different and deeper.

One journalist, after hearing the new Pope's first blessing in St. Peter's Square, wired back to his editors: "This is not a pope from Poland; this is a pope from Galilee." From that day to this, the Pope's life has written one of the great inspiring stories of our time.

We remember the Pope's first visit to Poland in 1979 when faith turned into resistance and began the swift collapse of imperial communism. The gentle, young priests, once ordered into forced labor by Nazis, became the foe of tyranny and a witness to hope.

The last leader of the Soviet Union would call him "the highest moral authority on earth." We remember his visit to a prison, comforting the man who shot him. By answering violence with forgiveness, the Pope became a symbol of reconciliation.

We remember the Pope's visit to Manila in 1995, speaking to one of the largest crowds in history, more than 5 million men and women and children. We remember that as a priest 50 years ago, he traveled by horse-cart to teach the children of small villages. Now he's kissed the ground of 123 countries and leads a flock of 1 billion into the Third Millennium.

We remember the Pope's visit to Israel and his mission of reconciliation and mutual respect between Christians and Jews. He is the first modern Pope to enter a synagogue or visit an Islamic country. He has always combined the practice of tolerance with a passion for truth.

John Paul himself has often said, "In the designs of Providence, there are no mere coincidences." And maybe the reason this man became Pope is that he bears the message our world needs to hear. To the poor, sick and dying he carries a message of dignity and solidarity with their suffering. Even when they are forgotten by men, he reminds them they are never forgotten by God.

"Do not give in to despair," he said, "in the South Bronx. God has your lives and His care goes with you, calls you to better things, calls you to overcome."

To the wealthy, this Pope carries the message that wealth alone is a false comfort. The goods of the world, he teaches, are nothing without goodness. We are called, each and every one of us, not only to make our own way, but to ease the path of others.

To those with power, the Pope carries a message of justice and human rights. And that message has caused dictators to fear and to fall. His is not the power of armies or technology or wealth. It is the unexpected power of a baby in a stable, of a man on a cross, of a simple fisherman who carried a message of hope to Rome.

Pope John Paul II brings that message of liberation to every corner of the world. When he arrived in Cuba in 1998, he was greeted by signs that read, "Fidel is the Revolution!" But as the Pope's biographer put it, "In the next four days Cuba belonged to another revolutionary." We are confident that the revolution of hope the Pope began in that nation will bear fruit in our time.

And we're responsible to stand for human dignity and religious freedom wherever they are denied, from Cuba to China to Southern Sudan. And we, in our country, must not ignore the words the Pope addresses to us. On his four pilgrimages to America, he has spoken with wisdom and feeling about our strengths and our flaws, our successes and our needs.

The Pope reminds us that while freedom defines our nation, responsibility must define our lives. He challenges us to live up to our aspirations, to be a fair and just society where all are welcomed, all are valued, and all are protected. And he is never more eloquent than when he speaks for a culture of life. The culture of life is a welcoming culture, never excluding, never dividing, never despairing and always affirming the goodness of life in all its seasons.

In the culture of life we must make room for the stranger. We must comfort the sick. We must care for the aged. We must welcome the immigrant. We must teach our children to be gentle with one another. We must defend in love the innocent child waiting to be born.

The center we dedicate today celebrates the Pope's message, its comfort and its challenge. This place stands for the dignity of the human person, the value of every life and the splendor of truth. And, above all, it stands, in the Pope's words, for the "joy of faith in a troubled world."

I'm grateful that Pope John Paul II chose Washington as the site of this center. It brings honor and it fills a need. We are thankful for the message. We are also thankful for the messenger, for his personal warmth and prophetic strength; for his good humor and his bracing honesty; for his spiritual and intellectual gifts; for his moral courage, tested against tyranny and against our own complacency.

Always, the Pope points us to the things that last and the love that saves. We thank God for this rare man, a servant of God and a hero of history. And I thank all of you for building this center of conscience and reflection in our Nation's Capital.

God bless.

On American Values

We hold dear what our Declaration of Independence says, that all have got uninalienable rights, endowed by a Creator — not endowed by the ones who wrote the Declaration of Independence, but by a Creator, a universal Creator.

–May 24, 2002

Our nation stands for freedom. That's what we're fighting off the terrorists about. We believe so strongly in freedom, we're willing to defend it at all costs. The Soviet era is gone. The Cold War, I hope, is past us. And today, President Putin and I signed an historic document. It was more than just a document that reduces nuclear weaponry, although that in itself is good. It's a document that says there's a new era ahead of us; that instead of being stuck in the past, these two leaders are willing to take two great countries forward in a new relationship built on common interests and cooperation. And cooperation on all fronts — the idea of working together to make the Russian economy strong and vibrant, so people can make a living, so people have hope about putting bread on the table for their families. The cooperation of fighting terror, the cooperation of promoting peace. But the best cooperation also must be based on common values, as well as common interests.

And I want you to know that we hold the values in America dear, and you know that. We hold dear what our Declaration of Independence says, that all have got uninalienable rights, endowed by a Creator — not endowed by the ones who wrote the Declaration of Independence, but by a Creator, a universal Creator. I want you to know that I believe all governments have a duty and responsibility to protect those rights, those inalienable rights.

In Soviet times, people heroically defended those rights with incredible courage, and you earned the respect of a lot of people — a lot of people — by doing so. Many of you now are active in a modern Russia, and I want to thank you for staying active and involved in this important society, starting with making sure that freedom is protected by rule of law, and we agree completely. And we hope we can help, because rule of law is essential for a modern society to thrive and to succeed.

I applaud your commitment and your patriotism. I love the fact that you love your country. I love mine and you love yours, and that's incredibly healthy and important. You understand that free nations and a free Russia require strong civic and religious institutions committed to democratic values.

Russia's on the road to democracy, but it's important, as she does so, that she embrace the values inherent in democracy. In the past, I know you know that we have been committed to helping institutions which promote those values through direct government assistance, and we will continue to do so. We believe it's for the good of Russia. We believe it will help Russia develop in a way that will be — enable Russia to become a lasting friend. And that's what I'm interested in. I'm interested in friendship, and peace, and mutual development.

Most Russians want and expect what most Americans want and expect — and that's important for the Russian people and the American people to understand — a government — starting with a government that works for citizens, that represents everyday citizens, not a corrupt elite. And that's important.

People want a society ruled by law, not by special privilege, special circumstance, a law where people are treated equally, regardless of their religion, ethnicity, income level. In a multi-ethnic society, people must work toward tolerance, and reject extremism. It's important in America, just like it's important here in Russia. And this is a multi-ethnic society, to the credit of Russia, just like America is a multi-ethnic society, which makes our country strong. We're bound together by common values, and so can Russia be bound by the same values.

To reach these goals, societies need fair laws, and as importantly, fair enforcement of law. They need independent media that is respected by the government. I remind those who sometimes get frustrated with the media that, even in America, elected officials sometimes don't agree what's written about them. Maybe especially America, for all I know. But it's important for those of us who value democracy to promote an independent media.

Opposition parties must be free to associate and must be free to speak their minds. In order for a democracy to be strong, there has to be competition of ideas, a free discussion of ideas and an airing of philosophy in an open way. Freedom of religion and separation of church and state are so important, so important so that people can worship as they choose — Jews, Muslims and all Christians, and all religions.

Free societies have all got to meet the great challenges we face in ways consistent with values. That's what I'm here to tell you that's in my heart. That's what I want you to know about this administration — that we're not only committed to fighting terrorism, and we will, we are. We were under attack in America.

In Germany yesterday I said, September the 11th was just a fine — just as clear a dividing line in our history, in our nation's history, as Pearl Harbor. It was. America at one time was protected by two oceans; we seemed totally invulnerable to, for example, the wars that took place here in Russia or on the European Continent, all of a sudden found ourselves attacked — because we love freedom, because we respect religion, because we honor discourse. And you need to know that we're going to defend ourselves, and defend that which we hold dear, and at the same time, protect civilization itself.

But in Afghanistan, we've shown, I believe, how to do it, in a way that's commensurate with our values — that, on the one hand, we're plenty tough, and we will be. We've got a military we're going to use, if we need to, to defend freedom. But on the other hand, we delivered a lot of medicine and a lot of food. We hurt thinking not only that the children in Afghanistan could not go to school, we cried for the fact that people were starving in the country. We have rebuilt schools. We have also provided medicine and food.

Russia is building hospitals in Afghanistan. It's incredibly positive, we think. Nations are not only contributing military forces, but we're working to build a state that can function on her own, a state at peace in the neighborhood, and a state where people have got hope and a chance to survive, where moms and dads can raise their children in peace.

And that's important for you to know, as well. You know, a lot of times people talk about the tough talk. But you've got to understand, we also have got a soft heart when it comes to the human condition. Each individual matters to me. Each individual has got worth and dignity.

The experience in Afghanistan has taught us all that there's lessons to be learned about how to protect one's homeland and, at the same time, be respectful on the battlefield. And that lesson applies to Chechnya. The war on terror can be won and, at the same time, we have proven it's possible to respect the rights of the people in the territories, to respect the rights of the minorities.

We are — I represent a great nation, and Russia is a great nation. Both of us share a lot. We've got a big resource base. We've got people who are very smart. I remind Vladimir Putin that the great resource of Russia is the people of Russia. The resource of this country is the brain power of this country.

And when they get the system right, that encourages individual growth and entrepreneurship, that brain power is going to flourish, and so will commerce, and so will opportunity. And while that happens, both nations must respect the multi-ethnic character of our lands. That, too, makes us great. And how we promote that multi-ethnicity, and how we respect human rights is another way we'll be judged by history. We'll be judged by history on how we defend our freedoms. We'll be judged in history by how we help our people prosper and grow. And we'll be judged by history as to whether or not we defend the universal values that are right and just and true.

I want to thank you for that commitment to those values. I appreciate your stance for freedom. I appreciate your love of your country. I appreciate your understanding there is a universal and gracious God.

May God bless you all. May God bless Russia. And may God bless the United States. Thank you very much.

On School Choice

Our nation will not accept one education system for those who can afford to send their children to a school of their choice and for those who can't.
–JULY 1, 2002

We must work to make the American Dream reach into every single neighborhood all across America.

I believe that starts with making sure everybody gets a good education. Rod talked about the "no child left behind" legislation. Let me tell you what I think the bill says. I believe it says that our society must believe every child can learn, and that means we've set high standards. If you set low standards, guess what's going to happen? If you have low expectations, you know what's going to happen? We'll just give up on kids — see?

It's so much harder to, by the way, educate inner-city — some inner-city children. It's easy to walk into a classroom full of inner-city African Americans, for example, and say, you can't learn, we'll move you through.

Or how about classrooms full of children whose parents don't speak English as a first language — it's easy to quit on those kids. Heck, it's hard to educate a child whose parents don't speak English; why don't we just shuffle them through the system. That means you have low hopes, low standards, low expectations. We start with a different premise: Every child can learn, regardless of their circumstances. And we expect every single child to learn in America.

We said, yes, there's a role for funding, and we increased funding for Title I programs here in Cleveland by 23 percent. And that's good and that's important. We want to help the disadvantaged through funding. But Washington shouldn't be telling Cleveland how to run its school system. See, that's up to you all to figure out how to run your school system.

But we've instituted a new reform, and it's an important reform. It says, if you do receive the money, if you decide to take federal money, show us whether or not the children are learning, see. Show us whether or not expectations are being met.

I've heard it all — we can't test, we test too much. We test too much. We shouldn't test children whether they can read. See, all you do is teach to test. Listen, if you can teach a child to read, they can pass a test. You teach them to read, don't worry about the tests.

We need to know in America whether or not our children can read and write and add and subtract. That's what an accountability system is for. Not only do we need to know, but more importantly, the parents need to know whether or not the children can read and write and add and subtract.

And if we find they can't, something else has to

happen. We cannot allow our children to be trapped in schools that won't teach and won't change.

Starting this September, as many as 3.5 million students across America who attend failing schools will have different options, of transferring to another public school. It's part of being an accountable society. It's part of strengthening public education.

Listen, I think public education is one of the most important parts of democracy. In order to make sure the American Dream reaches every neighborhood, we've got to have good public schools all across America. We must.

So we've got to strengthen the public education system, by encouraging different opportunities if there's failure.

Low income students, as a result of the new bill, in chronically failing schools will now have access to after-school tutoring. The money follows the child and the parent can decide who provides the after-school tutoring.

There is not a single avenue to success. In order to achieve educational excellence for every child there's got to be a multiplicity of approaches. That's why I believe so strongly in local control of schools. The people of Cleveland and the state of Ohio decided that one of the approaches they wanted to take was to encourage a voucher system to be implemented. That was a local decision.

And the Supreme Court of the United States gave a great victory to parents and students throughout the nation by upholding the decisions made by local folks here in the city of Cleveland, Ohio.

It is a constructive approach to improving public

education. We're interested in aiming toward excellence for every child. And the voucher system is a part of the strategy to achieve that here in Cleveland. One of my jobs is to make sure that we continue to insist upon reform, to take this court decision and encourage others to make the same decision at the local level.

One way to do so is through tax credits, which is now in my budget. I urge Congress, when we debate how to improve public education, to pass the tax credit so parents will have more flexibility and more choices when it comes to the education of their children, particularly K through 12.

I also — the Supreme Court in 1954 declared that our nation cannot have two education systems. And that was the right decision. We can't have two systems, one for African Americans and one for whites. Last week, what's notable and important is that the Court declared that our nation will not accept one education system for those who can afford to send their children to a school of their choice and for those who can't. And that's just as historic.

I think by continuing to focus on high standards and results and local control of schools, we can all work together to make sure no child is left behind.

On Taxes

It's not the government's money,
it's the people's money.
–April 16, 2001

☆

The Internal Revenue Service asks our families in America a lot of questions: how much did you earn; did you move last year; how big is your mortgage payment. You know, the truth of the matter is, the IRS knows more about us than our neighbors do. In a lot of cases, they know more about us than our families do.

But while the tax system knows a lot about our citizens, there's a lot our citizens may not know about our tax system. In 2001, the federal government will take a bigger share of the U.S. economy in taxes than in any year since 1944. And I remind you, in 1944, we had 11.5 million people under arms.

The federal government will take more as a percentage of the national economy this year than it did during World War II, except for one year; more than any year of the Vietnam War or the Korean conflict; more than it took to win World War I or prevail in the Cold War.

Our country is at peace, but our government is charging wartime prices. Enough is enough. The American people deserve tax relief.

You often hear it said, we cannot afford tax relief. But even after adjusting for inflation, the U.S. government will collect twice as much income tax revenue in 2001 as it did in 1981. Enough is enough, folks. It's time to give our folks some tax relief in America.

During the budget debates in Washington, some members of Congress complained that they did not have enough money to spend, but in 2001 the income tax will yield $2 billion in revenues for each and every one of the 535 members of Congress. I think they should be able to get by on that. No, enough's enough. People in America deserve tax relief.

Thanks to the help of a lot of folks here and all around the country, tax relief is on the way. The American taxpayer won some important victories a couple of weeks ago. The House of Representatives voted in favor of a plan that I think is an important plan, $1.6 trillion in tax relief over the next 10 years. The Senate approved most of my tax plan, but wants the government to spend far more.

Some members of the Senate are, unfortunately, proving the point I make all across the country — if you send it, they will spend it. Federal discretionary spending rose by 8 percent in 2001. The Senate has just voted to increase the discretionary spending by another 8 percent in 2002. At that rate, federal discretionary spending will double by 2010. Think about that. If we keep spending at the pace the Senate wants, in only nine years' time, government operations will cost twice as much as they do today.

Now, senators are in their home states this week listening to the taxpayers. I hope Americans will send a clear message: excessive federal spending threatens economic vitality. What we want is a stronger economy, not larger federal government

There's a better way: increase discretionary spending by a moderate and responsible 4 percent — by the way, at a rate larger than inflation — and then reduces — and then reduce taxes for everyone who pays taxes.

My plan does not puncture the tax code with loopholes. It doesn't give special treatment to special interests. My plan targets only one interest, the public interest. It directs help to individuals and families and small businesses. It is a plan for real people, and it will help produce real prosperity.

Let me tell you a little bit about what tax relief means for American families. My plan, when fully implemented, returns about $1,600 to the typical family of four. Sixteen hundred dollars pays the typical mortgage for more than a month. Sixteen hundred dollars will buy the typical family nearly three months worth of groceries. Sixteen hundred dollars will fuel two cars for a year.

There are a lot of American mothers and dads who wake up in America today anxious over bills they have to pay. Their worries don't get any easier when the federal government takes more of their income in taxes than they pay for food, shelter and clothing. For families with children to raise and debts to pay, tax relief will lift burdens and ease worries.

For small businesses, tax relief means more customers and improved cash flow, more money to hire more workers, more money to expand benefits, more money to invest in new technology. Tax relief will create new jobs. Tax relief will generate new wealth. And tax relief will open new opportunities.

If you read some of the news accounts of this budget debate, if you listen to what some of the members of Congress say, you'd think that little of value can ever happen in America unless the government makes it happen. You'd think that when we return money to the taxpayers it evaporates into the air.

Let me tell you some of the things $1.6 trillion could mean to the private economy. It could buy 10 million new middle income homes. It could pay the tuitions of 26 million young people at a private college or university for four years each. It could purchase 76 million new automobiles. These are the kinds of things Americans do with their own money. And there are many others.

Just ask Tommy and Sharen Winfield, for example. They're watching via closed circuit here from Atlanta, Georgia. The Winfields have three children. Tommy has been working as an operating engineer at Children's Hospital of Atlanta for the past three years. They pay $1,380 in federal income taxes. Under my plan, they'd pay nothing.

I first met Tommy a few weeks ago, and we were having a round-table discussion about tax relief. I asked him whether he thought the relief would make a difference to his family — you see, there are some who say, $1,380, that's nothing, that's not enough money for anybody.

But let me tell you what Tommy said loud and

clear, and I hope the members of the United States Congress hear it. Tommy said, sir, if they don't believe you — meaning, whether or not tax relief means anything — then they should just ask me. One thousand three hundred and eighty dollars means a lot to Tommy. It means a lot to a lot of folks in America: those who are struggling with higher energy bills, because we hadn't had an energy policy; those who have got big credit card debts.

We've got the Brake family with us from Alexandria, Virginia, Kelly and Pam. One less son. They pay $4,000 in federal income tax. Under my plan, they will save $1,700. That's real money for this hard-working couple. They and their two sons, I can assure you, will find good use for that tax relief. And whatever they do, I strongly believe they will spend it better and more productively than the federal government can.

This is an important debate for our country. It's a debate about how to make sure our economy continues to grow. But it's really a debate about who do we trust. Who do those of us who have been honored to serve our country at the federal level, who do we trust with the people's money? Do we trust our government, or do we trust the people? I believe after we meet priorities — and we meet priorities by growing the discretionary budget by 4 percent — that we always have got to remember whose money it is we're talking about. It's not the government's money; it's the people's money.

And we've always got to remember, the role of government is not to create wealth. It's to create an environment in which the entrepreneur can flourish, in which the small business can grow to become a big business. That's the role of government. And that's why it's vital at this point in American history that we return money back to the people. Instead of returning money, we ought not to take it in the first place, with real meaningful tax relief.

I've learned that the people can make a big difference in a lot of debates, particularly the tax relief debate. We're making some pretty good progress. I saw a good Democrat Senator out of Georgia the other day. Max Cleland said that he is interested in — when he comes back, interested in supporting the $1.6 trillion plan. I think that's what he said. It certainly sounded like it to me. And that's a good sign. I appreciate the Senator going home and listening to the people.

You see, I think we've finally made the case that we can meet the obligations of the federal government, that we don't have to grow at 8 percent in order to meet obligations. We've also made the case that sending money back to the people is important for our economy and important for the American Dream. And I want to thank your help for it.

I want to invite all Americans to take a look at the budget plan, themselves. You can order the little book by calling 202-512-1800, and ask for the Citizen's Guide to the Federal Budget. Or you can download it for free at www.whitehouse.government.

It's important for you to follow your government closely. It's important for you to not let the filter decide what's reality and what's not reality. It's important to get the facts. And it's always important to understand that tax relief will stimulate creativity and enterprise for individual Americans.

I firmly believe tax relief means a better life in a more prosperous America. So let the members of Congress know when they come back that you're watching, that you care for what they do because it will affect your life in a positive way.

I can't thank you all enough for your support, and I can't thank you enough for letting me come by and make my case. God bless you all.

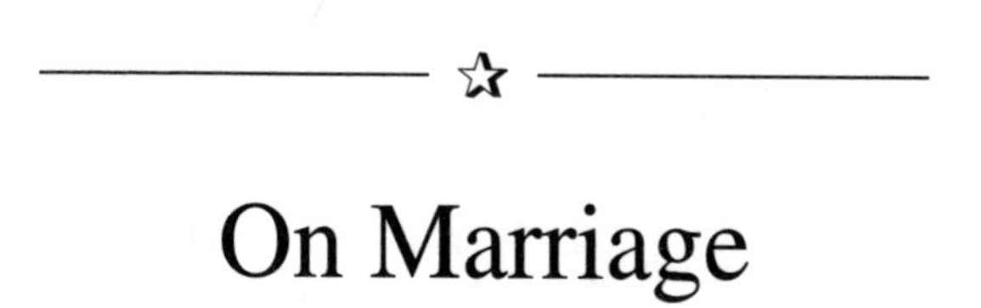

On Marriage

Marriage is a union between a man and a woman...
–OCTOBER 3, 2003

☆

Marriage is a sacred institution, and its protection is essential to the continued strength of our society. Marriage Protection Week provides an opportunity to focus our efforts on preserving the sanctity of marriage and on building strong and healthy marriages in America.

Marriage is a union between a man and a woman, and my Administration is working to support the institution of marriage by helping couples build successful marriages and be good parents.

To encourage marriage and promote the well-being of children, I have proposed a healthy marriage initiative to help couples develop the skills and knowledge to form and sustain healthy marriages. Research has shown that, on average, children raised in households headed by married parents fare better than children who grow up in other family structures. Through education and counseling programs, faith-based, community, and government organizations promote healthy marriages and a better quality of life for children. By supporting responsible child-rearing and strong families, my Administration is seeking to ensure that every child can grow up in a safe and loving home.

We are also working to make sure that the Federal Government does not penalize marriage. My tax relief package eliminated the marriage penalty. And as part of the welfare reform package I have proposed, we will do away with the rules that have made it more difficult for married couples to move out of poverty.

We must support the institution of marriage and help parents build stronger families. And we must continue our work to create a compassionate, welcoming society, where all people are treated with dignity and respect.

On Independence

Religious liberty is more than the right to believe in God's love; it is the right to be an instrument of God's love.
–July 4, 2001

When Jefferson sat down to write, he was trying, he said, to place before mankind "the common sense of the subject." The common sense of the subject was that we should be free. And though great evils would linger, the world would never be the same after July 4, 1776. A wonderful country was born, and a revolutionary idea sent forth to all mankind: Freedom, not by the good graces of government, but as the birthright of every individual. Equality, not as a theory of philosophers, but by the design of our Creator. Natural rights, not for the few, not even for a fortunate many, but for all people in all place, in all times.

The world still echoes with the ideals of America's Declaration. Our ideals have been accepted in many countries, and bitterly opposed by tyrants. They are the mighty rock on which we have built our nation. They are the hope of all who are oppressed. They are the standard to which we hold others, and the standard by which we measure ourselves.

Our greatest achievements have come when we have lived up to these ideals. Our greatest tragedies have come when we have failed to uphold them.

When Abraham Lincoln wondered whether civil war was preferable to permanent slavery, he knew where to seek guidance. Speaking in Independence Hall, he said, "I have never had a feeling, politically, that did not spring from the sentiments embodied in the Declaration of Independence." The Declaration, Lincoln said, gave promise that in due time the weight would be lifted from the shoulders of all men and all should have an equal chance.

From the ideals in the Declaration came the laws and the Constitution, including the free exercise of religion. The Liberty Bell was originally cast to mark the 50th anniversary of William Penn's Charter of Privileges, the first guarantee of religious freedom in this commonwealth. Now, exactly three centuries after William Penn's charter, the founders would be pleased to see that we have respected this right of the people and the limitation on the government. They knew what dangers can follow when government either dictates or frustrates the exercise of religion.

Our founders would also be pleased to walk these streets again and to find, amid the problems of modern life, a familiar American spirit of faith and good works. They would see the signs of poverty and want, but also acts of great kindness and charity. They would see addiction and the wreckage it brings. But they would also see in the works of the religious groups and charities throughout this city the power that can rescue abandoned hopes and repair a broken life.

In a world very different from theirs they would see different kinds of hardships, fears, and suffering. Yet, they would also recognize the brotherly love that gave this city its name. Your Mayor and I have just come from an Independence Day celebration in North Philadelphia, organized by a great American named Herbert Lusk. Herb first came into prominence as an athlete. Today he is pastor of Greater Exodus Baptist Church. And its parishioners still like him. Herb's church is one of the hundreds of churches and synagogues and mosques in this city where worship of the Almighty is expressed in service to neighbors in need.

In every part of Philadelphia, caring people are doing the work of compassion. They teach boys and girls to read, as in a program called Youth Education for Tomorrow, where more than 20 faith-based literacy centers are producing great results for your city's children.

At the Jesus School in North Philadelphia, little Aneeisha Graham came a year ago, not knowing any letters of the alphabet. Today, at age 7, she reads at the 4th grade level. Aneeisha is with us today. It's great to see you, darling. Thank you for coming.

Other faith-based groups in this city operate shelters for the destitute and the homeless. They bring kindness and understanding to young women facing domestic violence or crisis pregnancies. They give time and attention to the children of prisoners. These are the kinds of citizens every society needs

— citizens who speak for the voiceless and feed the hungry and protect the weak and comfort the afflicted.

America's founding documents give us religious liberty in principle; these Americans show us religious liberty in action. Religious liberty is more than the right to believe in God's love; it is the right to be an instrument of God's love

Such work is beyond the reach of government, and beyond the role of government. And those who hold positions of power should not be wary or hostile toward faith-based charities, or other community groups which perform important and good works. We should welcome their conviction and contribution in all its diversity.

So today I call on the United States Congress to pass laws promoting and encouraging faith-based and community groups in their important public work, and to never discriminate against them.

These soldiers in the armies of compassion deserve our support. They often need our support, and by taking their side we act in the best interests and tradition of our country. Without churches and charities, many of our citizens who have lost hope would be left to their own struggles and their own faith. And as I well know, they are not the only ones whose lives can be changed and uplifted by the influence of faith in God.

The founding generation discerned in that faith the source of our own rights — a divine gift of dignity, found equally in every human life. Our nation has always been guided by a moral compass.

In every generation men and women have protested terrible wrongs and worked for justice — for the abolition of slavery, the triumph of civil rights; for the end of child labor, the equal treatment of women, and the protection of innocent life.

Not every reformer in our history has been religious, but many have been motivated by a scriptural vision in which "justice rolls down like waters and righteousness like an ever-flowing stream."

We welcome religion in our common life because it leads millions of Americans to serve their neighbor, and because it leads countless others to speak for justice — from African American churches to Catholic bishops. "Religious people," said Dr. Martin Luther King, "should not be the servant of the state, nor the master of the state, but the conscience of the state."

In my inaugural address, I asked Americans to seek a common good beyond their comfort; to serve their nation, beginning with their neighbor. Today I urge Americans to consider what contributions we all can make — and there's plenty work for us all. Every person can find another to help. Nearly every community of conscience and faith has more to share, and corporate and foundation America can give more and give wiser.

In this way, we all become more responsible citizens. And by extending to all the promise of America, we show an important kind of patriotism. Seventy-five years ago, our 30th president, the only president born on Independence Day, spoke words that apply to our time. Calvin Coolidge said, "We live in an age of science and of abounding accumulation of material things. These did not create our Declaration. Our Declaration created them. The things of the spirit come first."

On this 4th of July, 2001, a great anniversary of our nation's birth, and a great anniversary of religious liberty, we remember the ideals of America and the things of the spirit that sustain them.

The Liberty Bell has been mostly silent for two centuries. And during the Revolution, it was unseen, hidden under the floorboards of a church in Allentown. Yet, even in silence, it has always borne one message, cast for the ages with the words of the Old Testament: "Proclaim liberty throughout all the land, unto all the inhabitants thereof." In this place of history, we honor the first generation of Americans who followed those words. And we give thanks to the God who watched over our country then, and who watches to this very day.

Thank you, all. And may God bless America.

On Religious Conviction

We do not impose any religion;
we welcome all religions. We do not prescribe any prayer, we welcome all prayers.
–February 1, 2001

America's Constitution forbids a religious test for office, and that's the way it should be. An American president serves people of every faith, and serves some of no faith at all. Yet I have found my faith helps me in the service to people. Faith teaches humility. As Laura would say, I could use a dose occasionally. A recognition that we are small in God's universe, yet precious in His sight. It has sustained me in moments of success, and in moments of disappointment. Without it I would be a different person, and without it I doubt I'd be here today.

There are many experiences of faith in this room. But most of us share a belief that we are loved, and called to love; that our choices matter, now and forever; that there are purposes deeper than ambition and hopes greater than success. These beliefs shape our lives and help sustain the life of our nation. Men and women can be good without faith, but faith is a force of goodness. Men and women can be compassionate without faith, but faith often inspires compassion. Human beings can love without faith, but faith is a great teacher of love.

Our country, from its beginnings, has recognized the contribution of faith. We do not impose any religion; we welcome all religions. We do not prescribe any prayer, we welcome all prayers. This is the tradition of our nation, and it will be the standard of my administration. We will respect every creed. We will honor the diversity of our country and the deep convictions of our people.

There's a good reason why many in our nation embrace the faith tradition. Throughout our history people of faith have often been our nation's voice of conscience. The foes of slavery could appeal to the standard that all are created equal in the sight of our Lord. The civil rights movement had the same conviction on its side — that men and women bearing God's image should not be exploited and set aside, and treated as insignificant. The same impulse over the years has reformed prisons and mental institutions, hospitals, hospices, and homeless shelters.

The Reverend Martin Luther King, Jr., said this: "The church must be reminded that it is not the master or the servant of the state, but rather the conscience of the state." As in his case, that sometimes means defying the times, challenging old ways and old assumptions. This influence has made our nation more just and generous and decent. And our nation has need of that today.

Faith remains important to the compassion of our nation. Millions of Americans serve their neighbor because they love their God. Their lives are characterized by kindness and patience, and service to others. They do for others what no government really can ever do — no government program can really ever do: They provide love for another human being. They provide hope even when hope comes hard.

In my second week in office we have set out to promote the work of community and faith-based charities. We want to encourage the inspired, to help the helper. Government cannot be replaced by charities, but it can welcome them as partners instead of resenting them as rivals.

My administration will put the federal government squarely on the side of America's armies of compassion. Our plan will not favor religious institutions over non-religious institutions. As president, I'm interested in what is constitutional, and I'm interested in what works. The days of discriminating against religious institutions, simply because they are religious, must come to an end.

Faith is also important to the civility of our country. It teaches us not merely to tolerate one another, but to respect one another — to show a regard for different views and the courtesy to listen. This is essential to democracy. It is also the proper way to treat human beings created in the divine image.

We'll have our disagreements. Civility does not require us to abandon deeply held beliefs. Civility does not demand casual creeds and colorless convictions. Americans have always believed that civility and firm resolve could live easily with one another. But civility does mean that our public debate ought to be free from bitterness and anger, rancor and ill-will. We have an obligation to make our case, not to demonize our opponents. As the Book of James reminds us, fresh water and salt water cannot flow from the same spring.

I am under no illusion that civility will triumph in this city all at once. Old habits die hard — and sometimes they never die at all. I can only pledge to you this, that I will do my very best to promote civility, and ask for the same in return.

These are some of the crucial contributions of faith to our nation: justice, and compassion, and a civil and generous society. I thank you for displaying these values, and defending them, here in America and across the world. You strengthen the ties of friendship and the ties of nations. And I deeply appreciate your work.

I believe in the power of prayer. It's been said: "I would rather stand against the cannons of the wicked than against the prayers of the righteous." The prayers of a friend are one of life's most gracious gifts. My family and I are blessed by the prayers of countless Americans. Over the last several months, Laura and I have been touched by the number of people who come up and say, "We pray for you." Such comforting words. I hope Americans will continue to pray that everyone in my administration finds wisdom, and always remembers the common good.

When President Harry Truman took office in 1945, he said: "At this moment, I have in my heart a prayer. I ask only to be a good and faithful servant of my Lord and my people." This has been the prayer of many presidents, and it is mine today. God bless.

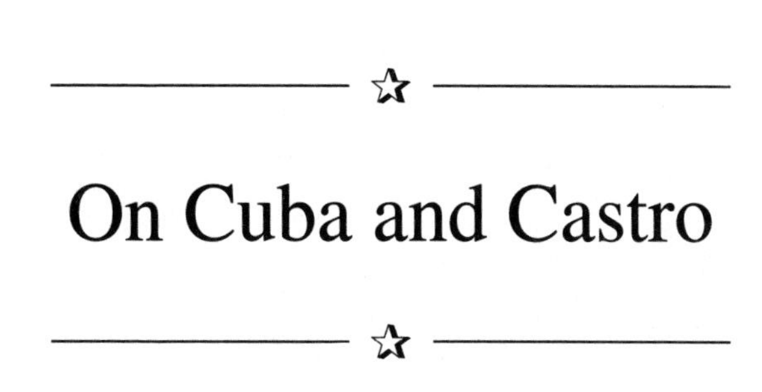

On Cuba and Castro

Viva Cuba Libre!
–MAY 20, 2002

Cuba's independence one century ago today was the inspiration of great figures such as Felix Varela. It was the result of determination and talent on the part of great statesmen such as Jose Marti, and great soldiers such as Antonio Maceo and Maximo Gomez. Most of all, Cuba's independence was the product of the great courage and sacrifice of the Cuban people.

Today, and every day for the past 43 years, that legacy of courage has been insulted by a tyrant who uses brutal methods to enforce a bankrupt vision. That legacy has been debased by a relic from another era, who has turned a beautiful island into a prison. In a career of oppression, Mr. Castro has imported nuclear-armed ballistic missiles, and he has exported his military forces to encourage civil war abroad.

He is a dictator who jails and tortures and exiles his political opponents. We know this. The Cuban people know this. And the world knows this. After all, just a month ago the United Nations Commission on Human Rights, in a resolution proposed by the nations of Latin America, called upon Cuba's government to finally — to finally — begin respecting the human rights of its people.

Through all their pains and deprivation, the Cuban people's aspirations for freedom are undiminished. We see this today in Havana, where more than 11,000 brave citizens have petitioned their government for a referendum on basic freedoms. If that referendum is allowed, it can be a prelude, a beginning for real change in Cuba.

The United States has no designs on Cuban sovereignty. It's not a part of our strategy, or a part of our vision. In fact, the United States has been a strong and consistent supporter of freedom for the Cuban people. And it is important for those who love freedom on that beautiful island to know that our support for them will never waver.

Today, I'm announcing an Initiative for a New Cuba that offers Cuba's government a way forward towards democracy and hope, and better relations with the United States.

Cuba's scheduled to hold elections to its National Assembly in 2003. Let me read Article 71 of the Cuban Constitution. It says, "The National Assembly is composed of deputies elected by free, direct, and secret vote." That's what the constitution says. Yet, since 1959, no election in Cuba has come close to meeting these standards. In most elections, there has been one candidate, Castro's candidate.

All elections in Castro's Cuba have been a fraud.

The voices of the Cuban people have been suppressed, and their votes have been meaningless. That's the truth. Es la verdad. In the 2003 National Assembly elections in Cuba, Cuba has the opportunity to offer Cuban voters the substance of democracy, not its hollow, empty forms.

Opposition parties should have the freedom to organize, assemble, and speak, with equal access to all airwaves. All political prisoners must be released and allowed to participate in the election process. Human rights organizations should be free to visit Cuba to ensure that the conditions for free elections are being created. And the 2003 elections should be monitored by objective outside observers. These are the minimum steps necessary to make sure that next year's elections are the true expression of the will of the Cuban people.

I also challenge Cuba's government to ease its stranglehold, to change its stranglehold on private economic activity. Political and economic freedoms go hand in hand, and if Cuba opens its political system, fundamental questions about its backward economic system will come into sharper focus.

If the Cuban government truly wants to advance the cause of workers, of Cuban workers, surely it will permit trade unions to exist outside of government control. If Cuba wants to create more good-paying jobs, private employers have to be able to negotiate with and pay workers of their own choosing, without the government telling who they can hire and who they must fire.

If Cuba wants to attract badly needed investment

from abroad, property rights must be respected. If the government wants to improve the daily lives of its people, goods and services produced in Cuba should be made available to all Cuban citizens. Workers employed by foreign companies should be paid directly by their employers, instead of having the government seize their hard-currency wages and pass on a pittance in the form of pesos. And the signs in hotels reading "Solamente Turistas" should finally be taken down.

Without major steps by Cuba to open up its political system and its economic system, trade with Cuba will not help the Cuban people. It's important for Americans to understand, without political reform, without economic reform, trade with Cuba will merely enrich Fidel Castro and his cronies.

Well-intentioned ideas about trade will merely prop up this dictator, enrich his cronies, and enhance the totalitarian regime. It will not help the Cuban people. With real political and economic reform, trade can benefit the Cuban people and allow them to share in the progress of our times.

If Cuba's government takes all the necessary steps to ensure that the 2003 elections are certifiably free and fair — certifiably free and fair — and if Cuba also begins to adopt meaningful market-based reforms, then — and only then — I will work with the United States Congress to ease the ban on trade and travel between our two countries.

Meaningful reform on Cuba's part will be answered with a meaningful American response. The goal of the United States policy toward Cuba is not a permanent embargo on Cuba's economy. The goal is freedom for Cuba's people.

Today's initiative invites the Cuban government to trust and respect Cuban citizens. And I urge other democracies, in this hemisphere and beyond, to use their influence on Cuba's government to allow free and fair National Assembly elections, and to push for real and meaningful and verifiable reform.

Full normalization of relations with Cuba — diplomatic recognition, open trade, and a robust aid program — will only be possible when Cuba has a new government that is fully democratic, when the rule of law is respected, and when the human rights of all Cubans are fully protected.

Yet, under the Initiative for a New Cuba, the United States recognizes that freedom sometimes grows step by step. And we'll encourage those steps. The current of history runs strongly towards freedom. Our plan is to accelerate freedom's progress in Cuba in every way possible, just as the United States and our democratic friends and allies did successfully in places like Poland, or in South Africa. Even as we seek to end tyranny, we will work to make life better for people living under and resisting Castro's rule.

Today I'm announcing a series of actions that will directly benefit the Cuban people, and give them greater control of their economic and political destiny. My administration will ease restrictions on humanitarian assistance by legitimate U.S. religious and other non-governmental organizations that directly serve the needs of the Cuban people and will help build Cuban civil society. And the United

States will provide such groups with direct assistance that can be used for humanitarian and entrepreneurial activities.

Our government will offer scholarships in the United States for Cuban students and professionals who try to build independent civil institutions in Cuba, and scholarships for family members of political prisoners. We are willing to negotiate direct mail service between the United States and Cuba.

My administration will also continue to look for ways to modernize Radio and TV Marti, because even the strongest walls of oppression cannot stand when the floodgates of information and knowledge are opened. And in the months ahead, my administration will continue to work with leaders all around our country, leaders who love freedom for Cuba, to implement new ways to empower individuals to enhance the chance for freedom.

The United States will continue to enforce economic sanctions on Cuba, and the ban on travel to Cuba, until Cuba's government proves that it is committed to real reform. We will continue to prohibit U.S. financing for Cuban purchases of U.S. agricultural goods, because this would just be a foreign aid program in disguise, which would benefit the current regime.

Today's initiative offers Cuba's government a different path, leading to a different future — a future of greater democracy and prosperity and respect. With real reform in Cuba, our countries can begin chipping away at four decades of distrust and division. And the choice rests with Mr. Castro.

Today, there is only one nation in our hemisphere that is not a democracy. Only one. There is only one national leader whose position of power owes more to bullets than ballots. Fidel Castro has a chance to escape this lonely and stagnant isolation. If he accepts our offer, he can bring help to his people and hope to our relations.

If Mr. Castro refuses our offer, he will be protecting his cronies at the expense of his people. And eventually, despite all his tools of oppression, Fidel Castro will need to answer to his people.

Jose Marti said, "Barriers of ideas are stronger than barricades of stone." For the benefit of Cuba's people, it is time for Mr. Castro to cast aside old and failed ideas and to start to think differently about the future. Today could mark a new dawn in a long friendship between our people, but only if the Castro regime sees the light.

Cuba's independence was achieved a century ago. It was hijacked nearly half a century ago. Yet the independent spirit of the Cuban people has never faltered. And it has never been stronger than it is today. The United States is proud to stand with all Cubans, and all Cuban-Americans, who love freedom. And we will continue to stand with you until liberty returns to the land you love so well.

Viva Cuba Libre.

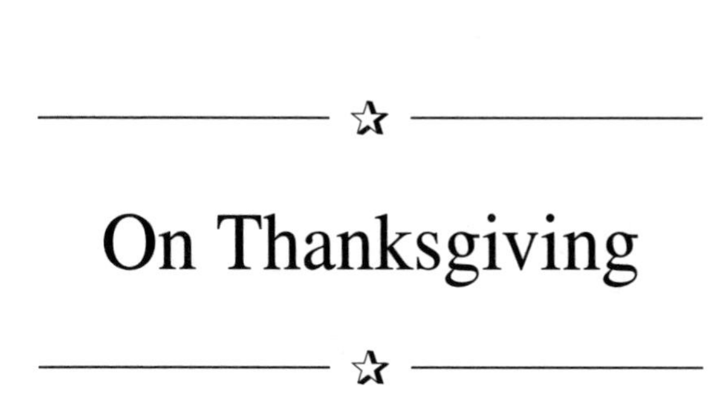

On Thanksgiving

I bring a message on behalf of America:
we thank you for your service, we're proud of you,
and America stands solidly behind you.
–NOVEMBER 27, 2003

Thank you. I was just looking for a warm meal somewhere. Thank you for inviting me to dinner. General Sanchez, thank you, sir, for your kind invitation and your strong leadership. Ambassador Bremer, thank you for your steadfast belief in freedom and peace. I want to thank the members of the Governing Council who are here, pleased you are joining us on our nation's great holiday; it's a chance to give thanks to the Almighty for the many blessings we receive.

I'm particularly proud to be with the 1st Armored Division, the 2nd ACR, the 82nd Airborne. I can't think of a finer group of folks to have Thanksgiving dinner with than you all. We're proud of you. Today, Americans are gathering with their loved ones to give thanks for the many blessings in our lives. And this year we are especially thankful for the courage and the sacrifice of those who defend us, the men and women of the United States military.

I bring a message on behalf of America: we thank you for your service, we're proud of you, and America stands solidly behind you. Together, you and I have taken an oath to defend our country. You're honoring that oath. The United States military is doing a fantastic job. You are defeating the terrorists here in Iraq, so that we don't have to face them in our own country. You're defeating Saddam's henchmen, so that the people of Iraq can live in peace and freedom.

By helping the Iraqi people become free, you're helping change a troubled and violent part of the world. By helping to build a peaceful and democratic country in the heart of the Middle East, you are defending the American people from danger, and we are grateful.

You're engaged in a difficult mission. Those who attack our coalition forces and kill innocent Iraqis are testing our will. They hope we will run. We did not charge hundreds of miles into the heart of Iraq, pay a bitter cost in casualties, defeat a brutal dictator and liberate 25 million people only to retreat before a band of thugs and assassins.

We will prevail. We will win because our cause is just. We will win because we will stay on the offensive. And we will win because you're part of the finest military ever assembled. And we will prevail because the Iraqis want their freedom.

Every day you see firsthand the commitment to sacrifice that the Iraqi people are making to secure their own freedom. I have a message for the Iraqi people: you have an opportunity to seize the moment and rebuild your great country, based on human dignity and freedom. The regime of Saddam Hussein is gone forever.

The United States and our coalition will help you, help you build a peaceful country so that your children can have a bright future. We'll help you find and bring to justice the people who terrorized you for years and are still killing innocent Iraqis. We will stay until the job is done. I'm confident we will succeed, because you, the Iraqi people, will show the world that you're not only courageous, but that you can govern yourself wisely and justly.

On this Thanksgiving, our nation remembers the men and women of our military, your friends and comrades who paid the ultimate price for our security and freedom. We ask for God's blessings on their families, their loved ones and their friends, and we pray for your safety and your strength, as you continue to defend America and to spread freedom.

Each one of you has answered a great call, participating in an historic moment in world history. You live by a code of honor, of service to your nation, with the safety and the security of your fellow citizens. Our military is full of the finest people on the face of the earth. I'm proud to be your Commander-in-Chief. I bring greetings from America. May God bless you all.

On America's Moral Compass

We seek the advance of freedom
and the peace that freedom brings.
–NOVEMBER 19, 2003

Americans traveling to England always observe more similarities to our country than differences. I've been here only a short time, but I've noticed that the tradition of free speech — exercised with enthusiasm — is alive and well here in London. We have that at home, too. They now have that right in Baghdad, as well.

The people of Great Britain also might see some familiar traits in Americans. We're sometimes faulted for a naive faith that liberty can change the world. If that's an error, it began with reading too much John Locke and Adam Smith. Americans have, on occasion, been called moralists who often speak in terms of right and wrong. That zeal has been inspired by examples on this island, by the tireless compassion of Lord Shaftesbury, the righteous courage of Wilberforce, and the firm determination of the Royal Navy over the decades to fight and end the trade in slaves.

It's rightly said that Americans are a religious people. That's, in part, because the "Good News" was translated by Tyndale, preached by Wesley, lived out in the example of William Booth. At times, Americans are even said to have a puritan streak — where might that have come from? Well, we can start with the Puritans.

To this fine heritage, Americans have added a few traits of our own: the good influence of our immigrants, the spirit of the frontier. Yet, there remains a bit of England in every American. So much of our national character comes from you, and we're glad for it.

The fellowship of generations is the cause of common beliefs. We believe in open societies ordered by moral conviction. We believe in private markets, humanized by compassionate government. We believe in economies that reward effort, communities that protect the weak, and the duty of nations to respect the dignity and the rights of all. And whether one learns these ideals in County Durham or in West Texas, they instill mutual respect and they inspire common purpose.

More than an alliance of security and commerce, the British and American peoples have an alliance of values. And, today, this old and tested alliance is very strong

The deepest beliefs of our nations set the direction of our foreign policy. We value our own civil rights, so we stand for the human rights of others. We affirm the God-given dignity of every person, so we are moved to action by poverty and oppression and famine and disease. The United States and Great Britain share a mission in the world beyond the balance of power or the simple pursuit of interest. We seek the advance of freedom and the peace that freedom brings. Together our nations are standing and sacrificing for this high goal in a distant land at this very hour. And America honors the idealism and the bravery of the sons and daughters of Britain.

The last president to stay at Buckingham Palace was an idealist, without question. At a dinner hosted by King George V, in 1918, Woodrow Wilson made a pledge; with typical American understatement, he vowed that right and justice would become the predominant and controlling force in the world.

President Wilson had come to Europe with his 14 Points for Peace. Many complimented him on his vision; yet some were dubious. Take, for example, the Prime Minister of France. He complained that God Himself had only 10 commandments. Sounds familiar.

At Wilson's high point of idealism, however, Europe was one short generation from Munich and Auschwitz and the Blitz. Looking back, we see the reasons why. The League of Nations, lacking both credibility and will, collapsed at the first challenge of the dictators. Free nations failed to recognize, much less confront, the aggressive evil in plain sight. And so dictators went about their business, feeding resentments and anti-Semitism, bringing death to innocent people in this city and across the world, and filling the last century with violence and genocide.

Through world war and cold war, we learned

that idealism, if it is to do any good in this world, requires common purpose and national strength, moral courage and patience in difficult tasks. And now our generation has need of these qualities.

On September the 11th, 2001, terrorists left their mark of murder on my country, and took the lives of 67 British citizens. With the passing of months and years, it is the natural human desire to resume a quiet life and to put that day behind us, as if waking from a dark dream. The hope that danger has passed is comforting, is understanding, and it is false. The attacks that followed — on Bali, Jakarta, Casablanca, Bombay, Mombassa, Najaf, Jerusalem, Riyadh, Baghdad, and Istanbul — were not dreams. They're part of the global campaign by terrorist networks to intimidate and demoralize all who oppose them.

These terrorists target the innocent, and they kill by the thousands. And they would, if they gain the weapons they seek, kill by the millions and not be finished. The greatest threat of our age is nuclear, chemical, or biological weapons in the hands of terrorists, and the dictators who aid them. The evil is in plain sight. The danger only increases with denial. Great responsibilities fall once again to the great democracies. We will face these threats with open eyes, and we will defeat them.

The peace and security of free nations now rests on three pillars: First, international organizations must be equal to the challenges facing our world, from lifting up failing states to opposing proliferation.

Like 11 presidents before me, I believe in the international institutions and alliances that America helped to form and helps to lead. The United States and Great Britain have labored hard to help make the United Nations what it is supposed to be — an effective instrument of our collective security. In recent months, we've sought and gained three additional resolutions on Iraq — Resolutions 1441, 1483 and 1511 — precisely because the global danger of terror demands a global response. The United Nations has no more compelling advocate than your Prime Minister, who at every turn has championed its ideals and appealed to its authority. He understands, as well, that the credibility of the U.N. depends on a willingness to keep its word and to act when action is required.

America and Great Britain have done, and will do, all in their power to prevent the United Nations from solemnly choosing its own irrelevance and inviting the fate of the League of Nations. It's not enough to meet the dangers of the world with resolutions; we must meet those dangers with resolve.

In this century, as in the last, nations can accomplish more together than apart. For 54 years, America has stood with our partners in NATO, the most effective multilateral institution in history. We're committed to this great democratic alliance, and we believe it must have the will and the capacity to act beyond Europe where threats emerge.

My nation welcomes the growing unity of Europe, and the world needs America and the European Union to work in common purpose for the advance of security and justice. America is cooperating with four other nations to meet the dangers posed by North Korea. America believes the IAEA must be true to its purpose and hold Iran to its obligations.

Our first choice, and our constant practice, is to work with other responsible governments. We understand, as well, that the success of multilateralism is not measured by adherence to forms alone, the tidiness of the process, but by the results we achieve to keep our nations secure.

The second pillar of peace and security in our world is the willingness of free nations, when the last resort arrives, to retain [sic] aggression and evil by force. There are principled objections to the use of force in every generation, and I credit the good motives behind these views.

Those in authority, however, are not judged only by good motivations. The people have given us the duty to defend them. And that duty sometimes requires the violent restraint of violent men. In some cases, the measured use of force is all that protects us from a chaotic world ruled by force.

Most in the peaceful West have no living memory of that kind of world. Yet in some countries, the memories are recent: The victims of ethnic cleansing in the Balkans, those who survived the rapists and the death squads, have few qualms when NATO applied force to help end those crimes. The women of Afghanistan, imprisoned in their homes and beaten in the streets and executed in public spectacles, did not reproach us for routing the Taliban. The inhabitants of Iraq's Baathist hell, with its lavish palaces and its torture chambers, with its massive statues and its mass graves, do not miss their fugitive dictator. They rejoiced at his fall.

In all these cases, military action was proceeded by diplomatic initiatives and negotiations and ultimatums, and final chances until the final moment. In Iraq, year after year, the dictator was given the chance to account for his weapons programs, and end the nightmare for his people. Now the resolutions he defied have been enforced.

And who will say that Iraq was better off when Saddam Hussein was strutting and killing, or that the world was safer when he held power? Who doubts that Afghanistan is a more just society and less dangerous without Mullah Omar playing host to terrorists from around the world. And Europe, too, is plainly better off with Milosevic answering for his crimes, instead of committing more.

It's been said that those who live near a police station find it hard to believe in the triumph of violence, in the same way free peoples might be tempted to take for granted the orderly societies we have come to know. Europe's peaceful unity is one of the great achievements of the last half-century. And because European countries now resolve differences through negotiation and consensus, there's sometimes an assumption that the entire world functions in the same way. But let us never forget how Europe's unity was achieved — by allied armies of liberation and NATO armies of defense. And let us never forget, beyond Europe's borders, in a world where oppression and violence are very real, liberation is still a moral goal, and freedom and security still need defenders.

The third pillar of security is our commitment to the global expansion of democracy, and the hope and progress it brings, as the alternative to instability and to hatred and terror. We cannot rely exclusively on military power to assure our long-term security. Lasting peace is gained as justice and democracy advance.

In democratic and successful societies, men and women do not swear allegiance to malcontents and murderers; they turn their hearts and labor to building better lives. And democratic governments do not shelter terrorist camps or attack their peaceful neighbors; they honor the aspirations and dignity of their own people. In our conflict with terror and tyranny, we have an unmatched advantage, a power that cannot be resisted, and that is the appeal of freedom to all mankind.

As global powers, both our nations serve the cause of freedom in many ways, in many places. By promoting development, and fighting famine and AIDS and other diseases, we're fulfilling our moral duties, as well as encouraging stability and building a firmer basis for democratic institutions. By working for justice in Burma, in the Sudan and in Zimbabwe, we give hope to suffering people and improve the chances for stability and progress. By extending the reach of trade we foster prosperity and the habits of liberty. And by advancing freedom in the greater Middle East, we help end a cycle of dictatorship and radicalism that brings millions of people to misery and brings danger to our own people.

The stakes in that region could not be higher. If

the Middle East remains a place where freedom does not flourish, it will remain a place of stagnation and anger and violence for export. And as we saw in the ruins of two towers, no distance on the map will protect our lives and way of life. If the greater Middle East joins the democratic revolution that has reached much of the world, the lives of millions in that region will be bettered, and a trend of conflict and fear will be ended at its source.

The movement of history will not come about quickly. Because of our own democratic development — the fact that it was gradual and, at times, turbulent — we must be patient with others. And the Middle East countries have some distance to travel.

Arab scholars speak of a freedom deficit that has separated whole nations from the progress of our time. The essentials of social and material progress — limited government, equal justice under law, religious and economic liberty, political participation, free press, and respect for the rights of women — have been scarce across the region. Yet that has begun to change. In an arc of reform from Morocco to Jordan to Qatar, we are seeing elections and new protections for women and the stirring of political pluralism. Many governments are realizing that theocracy and dictatorship do not lead to national greatness; they end in national ruin. They are finding, as others will find, that national progress and dignity are achieved when governments are just and people are free.

The democratic progress we've seen in the Middle East was not imposed from abroad, and neither will the greater progress we hope to see. Freedom, by definition, must be chosen, and defended by those who choose it. Our part, as free nations, is to ally ourselves with reform, wherever it occurs.

Perhaps the most helpful change we can make is to change in our own thinking. In the West, there's been a certain skepticism about the capacity or even the desire of Middle Eastern peoples for self-government. We're told that Islam is somehow inconsistent with a democratic culture. Yet more than half of the world's Muslims are today contributing citizens in democratic societies. It is suggested that the poor, in their daily struggles, care little for self-government. Yet the poor, especially, need the power of democracy to defend themselves against corrupt elites.

Peoples of the Middle East share a high civilization, a religion of personal responsibility, and a need for freedom as deep as our own. It is not realism to suppose that one-fifth of humanity is unsuited to liberty; it is pessimism and condescension, and we should have none of it.

We must shake off decades of failed policy in the Middle East. Your nation and mine, in the past, have been willing to make a bargain, to tolerate oppression for the sake of stability. Longstanding ties often led us to overlook the faults of local elites. Yet this bargain did not bring stability or make us safe. It merely bought time, while problems festered and ideologies of violence took hold.

As recent history has shown, we cannot turn a blind eye to oppression just because the oppression is not in our own backyard. No longer should we think tyranny is benign because it is temporarily convenient. Tyranny is never benign to its victims, and our great democracies should oppose tyranny wherever it is found.

Now we're pursuing a different course, a forward strategy of freedom in the Middle East. We will consistently challenge the enemies of reform and confront the allies of terror. We will expect a higher standard from our friends in the region, and we will meet our responsibilities in Afghanistan and in Iraq by finishing the work of democracy we have begun.

There were good-faith disagreements in your country and mine over the course and timing of military action in Iraq. Whatever has come before, we now have only two options: to keep our word, or to break our word. The failure of democracy in Iraq would throw its people back into misery and turn that country over to terrorists who wish to destroy us. Yet democracy will succeed in Iraq, because our will is firm, our word is good, and the Iraqi people will not surrender their freedom.

Since the liberation of Iraq, we have seen changes that could hardly have been imagined a year ago. A new Iraqi police force protects the people, instead of bullying them. More than 150 Iraqi newspapers are now in circulation, printing what they choose, not what they're ordered. Schools are open with textbooks free of propaganda. Hospitals are functioning and are well-supplied. Iraq has a new currency, the first battalion of a new army, representative local governments, and a Governing Council with an aggressive timetable for national sovereignty. This is substantial progress. And much of it has proceeded faster than similar efforts in Germany and Japan after World War II.

Yet the violence we are seeing in Iraq today is serious. And it comes from Baathist holdouts and Jihadists from other countries, and terrorists drawn to the prospect of innocent bloodshed. It is the nature of terrorism and the cruelty of a few to try to bring grief in the loss to many. The armed forces of both our countries have taken losses, felt deeply by our citizens. Some families now live with a burden of great sorrow. We cannot take the pain away. But these families can know they are not alone. We pray for their strength; we pray for their comfort; and we will never forget the courage of the ones they loved.

The terrorists have a purpose, a strategy to their cruelty. They view the rise of democracy in Iraq as a powerful threat to their ambitions. In this, they are correct. They believe their acts of terror against our coalition, against international aid workers and against innocent Iraqis, will make us recoil and retreat. In this, they are mistaken.

We did not charge hundreds of miles into the heart of Iraq and pay a bitter cost of casualties, and liberate 25 million people, only to retreat before a band of thugs and assassins. We will help the Iraqi people establish a peaceful and democratic country in the heart of the Middle East. And by doing so, we will defend our people from danger.

The forward strategy of freedom must also apply to the Arab-Israeli conflict. It's a difficult period in a part of the world that has known many. Yet, our commitment remains firm. We seek justice and dignity. We seek a viable, independent state for the Palestinian people, who have been betrayed by others for too long. We seek security and recognition for the state of Israel, which has lived in the shadow of random death for too long. These are worthy goals in themselves, and by reaching them we will also remove an occasion and excuse for hatred and violence in the broader Middle East.

Achieving peace in the Holy Land is not just a matter of the shape of a border. As we work on the details of peace, we must look to the heart of the matter, which is the need for a viable Palestinian democracy. Peace will not be achieved by Palestinian rulers who intimidate opposition, who tolerate and profit from corruption and maintain their ties to terrorist groups. These are the methods of the old elites, who time and again had put their own self-interest above the interest of the people they claim to serve. The long-suffering Palestinian people deserve better. They deserve true leaders, capable of creating and governing a Palestinian state.

Even after the setbacks and frustrations of recent months, goodwill and hard effort can bring about a Palestinian state and a secure Israel. Those who would lead a new Palestine should adopt peaceful means to achieve the rights of their people and create the reformed institutions of a stable democracy.

Israel should freeze settlement construction, dismantle unauthorized outposts, end the daily humiliation of the Palestinian people, and not prejudice final negotiations with the placements of walls and fences.

Arab states should end incitement in their own media, cut off public and private funding for terrorism, and establish normal relations with Israel.

Leaders in Europe should withdraw all favor and support from any Palestinian ruler who fails his people and betrays their cause. And Europe's leaders — and all leaders — should strongly oppose anti-Semitism, which poisons public debates over the future of the Middle East.

Ladies and gentlemen, we have great objectives before us that make our Atlantic alliance as vital as it has ever been. We will encourage the strength and effectiveness of international institutions. We will use force when necessary in the defense of freedom. And we will raise up an ideal of democracy in every part of the world. On these three pillars we will build the peace and security of all free nations in a time of danger.

So much good has come from our alliance of conviction and might. So much now depends on the strength of this alliance as we go forward. America has always found strong partners in London, leaders of good judgment and blunt counsel and backbone when times are tough. And I have found all those qualities in your current Prime Minister, who has my respect and my deepest thanks

The ties between our nations, however, are deeper than the relationship between leaders. These ties endure because they are formed by the experience and responsibilities and adversity we have shared. And in the memory of our peoples, there will always be one experience, one central event when the seal was fixed on the friendship between Britain and the United States: The arrival in Great Britain of more than 1.5 million American soldiers and airmen in the 1940s was a turning point in the Second World War. For many Britons, it was a first close look at Americans, other than in the movies. Some of you here today may still remember the "friendly invasion." Our lads, they took some getting used to. There was even a saying about what many of them were up to — in addition to be "overpaid and over here."

At a reunion in North London some years ago, an American pilot who had settled in England after his military service said, "Well, I'm still over here, and probably overpaid. So two out of three isn't bad."

In that time of war, the English people did get used to the Americans. They welcomed soldiers and flyers into their villages and homes, and took to calling them, "our boys." About 70,000 of those boys did their part to affirm our special relationship. They returned home with English brides.

Americans gained a certain image of Britain, as well. We saw an island threatened on every side, a leader who did not waver, and a country of the firmest character. And that has not changed. The British people are the sort of partners you want when serious work needs doing. The men and women of this Kingdom are kind and steadfast and generous and brave. And America is fortunate to call this country our closest friend in the world.

May God bless you all.

On Evil

One of the greatest Germans of the 20th century was Pastor Dietrich Bonhoeffer, who left the security of America to stand against Nazi rule. In a dark hour, he gave witness to the Gospel of life, and paid the cost of his discipleship, being put to death only days before his camp was liberated.

–MAY 23, 2002

And now I am honored to visit this great city. The history of our time is written in the life of Berlin. In this building, fires of hatred were set that swept across the world. To this city, Allied planes brought food and hope during 323 days and nights of siege. Across an infamous divide, men and women jumped from tenement buildings and crossed through razor wire to live in freedom or to die in the attempt. One American president came here to proudly call himself a citizen of Berlin. Another president dared the Soviets to "tear down that wall." And on a night in November, Berliners took history into their hands, and made your city whole.

In a single lifetime, the people of this capital and this country endured 12 years of dictatorial rule, suffered 40 years of bitter separation, and persevered through this challenging decade of unification. For all these trials, Germany has emerged a responsible, a prosperous and peaceful nation. More than a decade ago, as the president pointed out, my father spoke of Germany and America as partners in leadership — and this has come to pass. A new era has arrived — the strong Germany you have built is good for the world.

On both sides of the Atlantic, the generation of our fathers was called to shape great events — and they built the great transatlantic alliance of democracies. They built the most successful alliance in history. After the Cold War, during the relative quiet of the 1990s, some questioned whether our transatlantic partnership still had a purpose. History has given its answer. Our generation faces new and grave threats to liberty, to the safety of our people, and to civilization itself. We face an aggressive force that glorifies death, that targets the innocent, and seeks the means to matter — murder on a massive scale.

We face the global tragedy of disease and poverty that take uncounted lives and leave whole nations vulnerable to oppression and terror.

We'll face these challenges together. We must face them together. Those who despise human freedom will attack it on every continent. Those who seek missiles and terrible weapons are also familiar with the map of Europe. Like the threats of another era, this threat cannot be appeased or cannot be ignored. By being patient, relentless, and resolute, we will defeat the enemies of freedom

By remaining united, we are meeting — we are meeting modern threats with the greatest resources of wealth and will ever assembled by free nations. Together, Europe and the United States have the creative genius, the economic power, the moral heritage, and the democratic vision to protect our liberty and to advance our cause of peace.

Different as we are, we are building and defending the same house of freedom — its doors open to all of Europe's people, its windows looking out to global challenges beyond. We must lay the foundation with a Europe that is whole and free and at peace for the first time in its history. This dream of the centuries is close at hand.

From the Argonne Forest to the Anzio beachhead, conflicts in Europe have drawn the blood of millions, squandering and shattering lives across the earth. There are thousands, thousands of monuments in parks and squares across my country to young men of 18 and 19 and 20 whose lives ended in battle on this continent. Ours is the first generation in a hundred years that does not expect and does not fear the next European war. And that achievement — your achievement — is one of the greatest in modern times.

When Europe grows in unity, Europe and America grow in security. When you integrate your markets and share a currency in the European Union, you are creating the conditions for security and common purpose. In all these steps, Americans do not see the rise of a rival; we see the end of old hostilities. We see the success of our allies, and we applaud your progress.

The expansion of NATO will also extend the security on this continent, especially for nations that knew little peace or security in the last century. We have moved cautiously in this direction. Now we must act decisively.

As our summit in Prague approaches, America is committed to NATO membership for all of Europe's democracies that are ready to share in the responsibilities that NATO brings. Every part of Europe should share in the security and success of this continent. A broader alliance will strengthen NATO — it will fulfill NATO's promise.

Another mission we share is to encourage the Russian people to find their future in Europe and with America. Russia has its best chance since 1917 to become a part of Europe's family. Russia's transformation is not finished; the outcome is not yet determined. But for all the problems and challenges, Russia is moving toward freedom — more freedom in its politics and its markets; freedom that will help Russia to act as a great and a just power. A Russia at peace with its neighbors, respecting the legitimate rights of minorities, is welcome in Europe.

A new Russian-American partnership is being forged. Russia is lending crucial support in the war on global terror. A Russian colonel now works on the staff of U.S. Army General Tommy Franks, commander of the war in Afghanistan. And in Afghanistan itself, Russia is helping to build hospitals and a better future for the Afghan people.

America and Europe must throw off old suspicions and realize our common interests with Russia. Tomorrow in Moscow, President Putin and I will again act upon these interests.

The United States and Russia are ridding ourselves of the last vestiges of cold War confrontation. We have moved beyond an ABM treaty that prevented us from defending our people and our friends. Some warned that moving beyond the ABM treaty would cause an arms race. Instead, President Putin and I are about to sign the most dramatic nuclear arms reduction in history. Both the United States and Russia will reduce our nuclear arsenals by about two-thirds — to the lowest levels in decades.

Old arms agreements sought to manage hostility and maintain a balance of terror. This new agreement recognizes that Russia and the West are no longer enemies.

The entire transatlantic alliance is forming a new relationship with Russia. Next week in Rome, Chancellor Schroeder, NATO allies, and I will meet as equal partners with President Putin at the creation of the NATO-Russia Council. The Council gives us an opportunity to build common security against common threats. We will start with projects on nonproliferation, counterterrorism, and search-and-rescue operations. Over time, we will expand this cooperation, even as we preserve the core mission of NATO. Many generations have looked at Russia with alarm. Our generation can finally lift this shadow from Europe by embracing the friendship of a new democratic Russia.

As we expand our alliance, as we reach out to

Russia, we must also look beyond Europe to gathering dangers and important responsibilities. As we build the house of freedom, we must meet the challenges of a larger world. And we must meet them together.

For the United States, September the 11th, 2001, cut a deep dividing line in our history — a change of eras as sharp and clear as Pearl Harbor or the first day of the Berlin Blockade. There can be no lasting security in a world at the mercy of terrorists — for my nation, or for any nation.

Given this threat, NATO's defining purpose — our collective defense — is as urgent as ever. America and Europe need each other to fight and win the war against global terror. My nation is so grateful for the sympathy of the German people, and for the strong support of Germany and all of Europe.

Troops from more than a dozen European countries have deployed in and around Afghanistan, including thousands from this country — the first deployment of German forces outside of Europe since 1945. German soldiers have died in this war, and we mourn their loss as we do our own. German authorities are on the trail of terrorist cells and finances. And German police are helping Afghans build their own police force. And we're so grateful for the support.

Together, we oppose an enemy that thrives on violence and the grief of the innocent. The terrorists are defined by their hatreds: they hate democracy and tolerance and free expression and women and Jews and Christians and all Muslims who disagree with them. Others killed in the name of racial purity or the class struggle. These enemies kill in the name of a false religious purity, perverting the faith they claim to hold. In this war we defend not just America or Europe; we are defending civilization itself.

The evil that has formed against us has been termed the "new totalitarian threat." The authors of terror are seeking nuclear, chemical and biological weapons. Regimes that sponsor terror are developing these weapons and the missiles to deliver them. If these regimes and their terrorist allies were to perfect these capabilities, no inner voice of reason, no hint of conscience would prevent their use.

Wishful thinking might bring comfort, but not security. Call this a strategic challenge; call it, as I do, axis of evil; call it by any name you choose, but let us speak the truth. If we ignore this threat, we invite certain blackmail, and place millions of our citizens in grave danger.

Our response will be reasoned, and focused, and deliberate. We will use more than our military might. We will cut off terrorist finances, apply diplomatic pressure, and continue to share intelligence. America will consult closely with our friends and allies at every stage. But make no mistake about it, we will and we must confront this conspiracy against our liberty and against our lives.

As it faces new threats, NATO needs a new strategy and new capabilities. Dangers originating far from Europe can now strike at Europe's heart — so NATO must be able and willing to act whenever threats emerge. This will require all the assets of modern defense — mobile and deployable forces, sophisticated special operations, the ability to fight under the threat of chemical and biological weapons. Each nation must focus on the military strengths it can bring to this alliance, with the hard choices and financial commitment that requires. We do not know where the next threat might come from; we really don't know what form it might take. But we must be ready, as full military partners, to confront threats to our common security.

One way to make ourselves more secure is to address the regional conflicts that enflame violence. Our work in the Balkans and Afghanistan shows how much we can achieve when we stand together. We must continue to stand for peace in the Middle East. That peace must assure the permanent safety of the Jewish people. And that peace must provide the Palestinian people with a state of their own.

In the midst of terrorist violence in the Middle East, the hope of a lasting accord may seem distant. That's how many once viewed the prospect of peace between Poland and Germany, Germany and France, France and England, Protestant and Catholic. Yet, after generations of traded violence and humiliation, we have seen enemies become partners and allies in a new Europe. We pray the same healing, the same shedding of hatred, might come to the Middle East. And we will be unrelenting in our quest for that peace.

We must recognize that violence and resentment are defeated by the advance of health, and learning, and prosperity. Poverty doesn't create terror — yet, terror takes root in failing nations that cannot police themselves or provide for their people. Our conscience and our interests speak as one: to achieve a safer world, we must create a better world.

The expansion of trade in our time is one of the primary reasons for our progress against poverty. At Doha, we committed to build on this progress, and we must keep that commitment. Trans-Atlantic nations must resolve the small, disputed portion of our vast trading relationship within the rules and settlement mechanisms of the World Trade Organization — whether those disputes concern tax law, steel, agricultural or biotechnology.

For all nations — for all nations to gain the benefit of global markets, they need populations that are healthy and literate. To help developing nations achieve these goals, leaders of wealthy nations have a duty of conscience. We have a duty to share our wealth generously and wisely. Those who lead poor nations have a duty to their own people — but they have a duty as well: to pursue reforms that turn temporary aid into lasting progress.

I've proposed that new American aid be directed to nations on that path of reform. The United States will increase our core development assistance by 50 percent over the next three budget years. It will be up to a level of $5 billion a year, above and beyond that which we already contribute to development.

When nations are governed justly, the people benefit. When nations are governed unjustly, for the benefit of a corrupt few, no amount of aid will help the people in need. When nations are governed justly — when nations are governed justly, investing in education and health, and encouraging economic freedom, they will have our help. And more importantly, these rising nations will have their own ability and, eventually, the resources necessary to battle disease and improve their environment, and build lives of dignity for their people.

Members of the Bundestag, we are joined in serious purpose — very serious purposes — on which the safety of our people and the fate of our freedom now rest. We build a world of justice, or we will live in a world of coercion. The magnitude of our shared responsibilities makes our disagreements look so small. And those who exaggerate our differences play a shallow game and hold a simplistic view of our relationship.

America and the nations in Europe are more than military allies, we're more than trading partners; we are heirs to the same civilization. The pledges of the Magna Carta, the learning of Athens, the creativity of Paris, the unbending conscience of Luther, the gentle faith of St. Francis — all of these are part of the American soul. The New World has succeeded by holding to the values of the Old.

Our histories have diverged, yet we seek to live by the same ideals. We believe in free markets, tempered by compassion. We believe in open societies that reflect unchanging truths. We believe in the value and dignity of every life.

These convictions bind our civilization together and set our enemies against us. These convictions are universally true and right. And they define our nations and our partnership in a unique way. And these beliefs lead us to fight tyranny and evil, as others have done before us.

One of the greatest Germans of the 20th century was Pastor Dietrich Bonhoeffer, who left the security of America to stand against Nazi rule. In a dark hour, he gave witness to the Gospel of life, and paid the cost of his discipleship, being put to death only days before his camp was liberated.

"I believe," said Bonhoeffer, "that God can and wants to create good out of everything, even evil."

That belief is proven in the history of Europe since that day — in the reconciliation and renewal that have transformed this continent. In America, very recently, we have also seen the horror of evil and the power of good. In the tests of our time, we are affirming our deepest values and our closest friendships. Inside this chamber, across this city, throughout this nation and continent, America has valued friends. And with our friends we are building that house of freedom — for our time and for all time.

May God bless.

On Justice

...you have reminded America that we have a special calling to promote justice and to defend the weak and suffering of the world. We remember your words, and we will always do our best to remember our calling.

–July 23, 2001

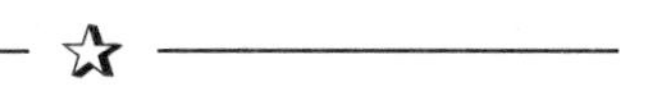

HIS HOLINESS POPE JOHN PAUL II:

Mr. President, it gives me great pleasure to welcome you on your first visit since you assumed the office of the President of the United States. I warmly greet the distinguished First Lady and the members of your entourage. I express heartfelt good wishes that your presidency will strengthen your country in its commitment to the principles which inspired American democracy from the beginning, and sustained the nation and its remarkable growth. These principles remain as valid as ever as you face the challenges of the new country opening up before us.

Your nation's founders, conscious of the immense natural and human resources with which your land has been blessed by the Creator, were guided by a profound sense of responsibility towards the common good to be pursued in respect for the God-given dignity and inalienable rights of all. America continues to measure herself by the nobility of her founding vision in building this society of liberty, equality and justice under the law. In the century which has just ended, these same ideals inspired the American people to resist two totalitarian systems, based on an atheistic vision of man and society.

At the beginning of this new century, which also marks the beginning of the third millennium of Christianity, the world continues to look to America with hope. And it does so with an acute awareness of the crisis of values being experienced in Western society, ever more insecure in the face of the ethical decisions, indispensable for humanity's future course.

In recent days, the world's attention has been focused on the process of globalization which has so greatly accelerated in the past decade, and which you and other leaders of the industrialized nations have discussed in Genoa. While appreciating the opportunities for economic growth and material prosperity, which this process offers, the Church cannot but express profound concern that our world continues to be divided no longer by the former political and military blocs, but by a tragic fault-line between those who can benefit from these opportunities and those who seem cut off from them.

The revolution of freedom of which I spoke at the United Nations in 1995 must now be completed by a revolution of opportunity, in which all the world's people actively contribute to the economic prosperity and share in its fruits. This requires leadership by those nations whose religious and cultural traditions should make them most attentive to the moral dimension of the issues involved.

Respect for human dignity and belief in the equal dignity of all the members of the human family demand policies aimed at enabling all people to access to the means required to improve their lives, including the technological means and skills needed for development. Respect for nature by everyone, a policy of openness to immigrants, the cancellation or significant reduction of the debt of poorer nations, the promotion of peace through dialogue and negotiation, the primacy of the rule of law — these are the priorities which the leaders of the developed countries cannot disregard. A global world is essentially a world of solidarity. From this point of view, America, because of her many resources, cultural traditions and religious values, has a special responsibility.

Respect for human dignity finds one of its highest expressions in religious freedom. This right is the first listed in your nation's Bill of Rights, and it is significant that the promotion of religious freedom continues to be an important goal of American policy in the international community. I want to express the appreciation of the whole Catholic Church for America's commitment in this regard.

Another area in which political and moral choices have the gravest consequences for the future of civilization concerns the most fundamental of human rights, the right to life itself. Experience is already showing how a tragic coarsening of consciences accompanies the assault on innocent human life in the womb, leading to accommodation and acquiescence in the face of other related evils, such as euthanasia, infanticide, and most recently, proposals for the creation for research purposes of human embryos, destined to destruction in the process.

A free and virtuous society, which America aspires to be, must reject practices that devalue and violate human life at any stage from conception until natural death. In defending the right to life, in law and through a vibrant culture of life, America can show a world the path to a truly humane future in which man remains the master, not the product of his technology.

Mr. President, as you carry out the tasks of the high office which the American people have entrusted to you, I assure you of a remembrance in my prayers. I am confident that under your leadership, your nation will continue to draw on its heritage and resources to help build a world in which each member of the human family can flourish and live in a manner worthy of his or her innate dignity. With these sentiments, I cordially invoke upon you and the beloved American people God's blessings of wisdom, strength and peace.

PRESIDENT BUSH:

Your Holiness, thank you very much. Mrs. Bush and I are honored to stand with you today. We're grateful for your welcome. You've been to America many times, and have spoken to vast crowds. You have met with four American presidents before me, including my father. In every visit, and in every meeting, including our meeting today, you have reminded America that we have a special calling to promote justice and to defend the weak and suffering of the world. We remember your words, and we will always do our best to remember our calling.

Since October of 1978, you have shown the world not only the splendor of truth, but also the power of truth to overcome evil and to redirect the course of history. You have urged men and women of goodwill to take to their knees before God, and to stand unafraid before tyrants. And this has added greatly to the momentum of freedom in our time.

Where there's oppression, you speak of human rights. Where there's poverty, you speak of justice and hope. Where there's ancient hatred, you defend and display a tolerance that reaches beyond every boundary of race and nation and belief. Where there's great abundance, you remind us that wealth must be matched with compassion and moral purpose. And always, to all, you have carried the Gospel of life, which welcomes the stranger and protects the weak and the innocent. Every nation, including my own, benefits from hearing and heeding this message of conscience.

Above all, you have carried the message of the Gospel into 126 nations, and into the third millennium, always with courage and with confidence. You have brought the love of God into the lives of men, and that good news is needed in every nation and every age.

On Duty

We cannot defend America and our friends
by hoping for the best.
–June 1, 2002

☆

History has also issued its call to your generation. In your last year, America was attacked by a ruthless and resourceful enemy. You graduate from this Academy in a time of war, taking your place in an American military that is powerful and is honorable. Our war on terror is only begun, but in Afghanistan it was begun well.

I am proud of the men and women who have fought on my orders. America is profoundly grateful for all who serve the cause of freedom, and for all who have given their lives in its defense. This nation respects and trusts our military, and we are confident in your victories to come.

This war will take many turns we cannot predict. Yet I am certain of this: Wherever we carry it, the American flag will stand not only for our power, but for freedom. Our nation's cause has always been larger than our nation's defense. We fight, as we always fight, for a just peace — a peace that favors human liberty. We will defend the peace against threats from terrorists and tyrants. We will preserve the peace by building good relations among the great powers. And we will extend the peace by encouraging free and open societies on every continent.

Building this just peace is America's opportunity and America's duty. From this day forward, it is your challenge as well, and we will meet this challenge together. You will wear the uniform of a great and unique country. America has no empire to extend or utopia to establish. We wish for others only what we wish for ourselves — safety from violence, the rewards of liberty, and the hope for a better life.

In defending the peace, we face a threat with no precedent. Enemies in the past needed great armies and great industrial capabilities to endanger the American people and our nation. The attacks of September the 11th required a few hundred thousand dollars in the hands of a few dozen evil and deluded men. All of the chaos and suffering they caused came at much less than the cost of a single tank. The dangers have not passed. This government and the American people are on watch. We are ready, because we know the terrorists have more money and more men and more plans.

The gravest danger to freedom lies at the perilous crossroads of radicalism and technology. When the spread of chemical and biological and nuclear weapons, along with ballistic missile technology — when that occurs, even weak states and small groups could attain a catastrophic power to strike great nations. Our enemies have declared this very intention, and have been caught seeking these terrible weapons. They want the capability to blackmail us, or to harm us, or to harm our friends — and we will oppose them with all our power.

For much of the last century, America's defense relied on the Cold War doctrines of deterrence and containment. In some cases, those strategies still apply. But new threats also require new thinking. Deterrence — the promise of massive retaliation against nations — means nothing against shadowy terrorist networks with no nation or citizens to defend. Containment is not possible when unbalanced dictators with weapons of mass destruction can deliver those weapons on missiles or secretly provide them to terrorist allies.

We cannot defend America and our friends by hoping for the best. We cannot put our faith in the word of tyrants, who solemnly sign non-proliferation treaties, and then systemically break them. If we wait for threats to fully materialize, we will have waited too long.

Homeland defense and missile defense are part of stronger security, and they're essential priorities for America. Yet the war on terror will not be won on the defensive. We must take the battle to the enemy, disrupt his plans, and confront the worst threats before they emerge. In the world we have entered, the only path to safety is the path of action. And this nation will act.

Our security will require the best intelligence, to reveal threats hidden in caves and growing in laboratories. Our security will require modernizing domestic agencies such as the FBI, so they're prepared to act, and act quickly, against danger. Our security will require transforming the military you will lead — a military that must be ready to strike at a moment's notice in any dark corner of the world. And our security will require all Americans to be forward-looking and resolute, to be ready for preemptive action when necessary to defend our liberty and to defend our lives.

The work ahead is difficult. The choices we will face are complex. We must uncover terror cells in 60 or more countries, using every tool of finance, intelligence and law enforcement. Along with our friends and allies, we must oppose proliferation and confront regimes that sponsor terror, as each case requires. Some nations need military training to fight terror, and we'll provide it. Other nations oppose terror, but tolerate the hatred that leads to terror — and that must change. We will send diplomats where they are needed, and we will send you, our soldiers, where you're needed.

All nations that decide for aggression and terror will pay a price. We will not leave the safety of America and the peace of the planet at the mercy of a few mad terrorists and tyrants. We will lift this dark threat from our country and from the world.

Because the war on terror will require resolve and patience, it will also require firm moral purpose. In this way our struggle is similar to the Cold War. Now, as then, our enemies are totalitarians, holding a creed of power with no place for human dignity.

Now, as then, they seek to impose a joyless conformity, to control every life and all of life.

America confronted imperial communism in many different ways — diplomatic, economic, and military. Yet moral clarity was essential to our victory in the Cold War. When leaders like John F. Kennedy and Ronald Reagan refused to gloss over the brutality of tyrants, they gave hope to prisoners and dissidents and exiles, and rallied free nations to a great cause.

Some worry that it is somehow undiplomatic or impolite to speak the language of right and wrong. I disagree. Different circumstances require different methods, but not different moralities. Moral truth is the same in every culture, in every time, and in every place. Targeting innocent civilians for murder is always and everywhere wrong. Brutality against women is always and everywhere wrong. There can be no neutrality between justice and cruelty, between the innocent and the guilty. We are in a conflict between good and evil, and America will call evil by its name. By confronting evil and lawless regimes, we do not create a problem, we reveal a problem. And we will lead the world in opposing it.

As we defend the peace, we also have an historic opportunity to preserve the peace. We have our best chance since the rise of the nation state in the 17th century to build a world where the great powers compete in peace instead of prepare for war. The history of the last century, in particular, was dominated by a series of destructive national rivalries that left battlefields and graveyards across the Earth.

Germany fought France, the Axis fought the Allies, and then the East fought the West, in proxy wars and tense standoffs, against a backdrop of nuclear Armageddon.

Competition between great nations is inevitable, but armed conflict in our world is not. More and more, civilized nations find ourselves on the same side — united by common dangers of terrorist violence and chaos. America has, and intends to keep, military strengths beyond challenge — thereby making the destabilizing arms races of other eras pointless, and limiting rivalries to trade and other pursuits of peace.

Today the great powers are also increasingly united by common values, instead of divided by conflicting ideologies. The United States, Japan and our Pacific friends, and now all of Europe, share a deep commitment to human freedom, embodied in strong alliances such as NATO. And the tide of liberty is rising in many other nations.

Generations of West Point officers planned and practiced for battles with Soviet Russia. I've just returned from a new Russia, now a country reaching toward democracy, and our partner in the war against terror. Even in China, leaders are discovering that economic freedom is the only lasting source of national wealth. In time, they will find that social and political freedom is the only true source of national greatness.

When the great powers share common values, we are better able to confront serious regional conflicts together, better able to cooperate in preventing the spread of violence or economic chaos. In the past, great power rivals took sides in difficult regional problems, making divisions deeper and more complicated. Today, from the Middle East to South Asia, we are gathering broad international coalitions to increase the pressure for peace. We must build strong and great power relations when times are good; to help manage crisis when times are bad. America needs partners to preserve the peace, and we will work with every nation that shares this noble goal.

And finally, America stands for more than the absence of war. We have a great opportunity to extend a just peace, by replacing poverty, repression, and resentment around the world with hope of a better day. Through most of history, poverty was persistent, inescapable, and almost universal. In the last few decades, we've seen nations from Chile to South Korea build modern economies and freer societies, lifting millions of people out of despair and want. And there's no mystery to this achievement.

The 20th century ended with a single surviving model of human progress, based on non-negotiable demands of human dignity, the rule of law, limits on the power of the state, respect for women and private property and free speech and equal justice and religious tolerance. America cannot impose this vision — yet we can support and reward governments that make the right choices for their own people. In our development aid, in our diplomatic efforts, in our international broadcasting, and in our educational assistance, the United States will promote moderation and tolerance and human rights. And we will defend the peace that makes all progress possible.

When it comes to the common rights and needs of men and women, there is no clash of civilizations. The requirements of freedom apply fully to Africa and Latin America and the entire Islamic world. The peoples of the Islamic nations want and deserve the same freedoms and opportunities as people in every nation. And their governments should listen to their hopes.

A truly strong nation will permit legal avenues of dissent for all groups that pursue their aspirations without violence. An advancing nation will pursue economic reform, to unleash the great entrepreneurial energy of its people. A thriving nation will respect the rights of women, because no society can prosper while denying opportunity to half its citizens. Mothers and fathers and children across the Islamic world, and all the world, share the same fears and aspirations. In poverty, they struggle. In tyranny, they suffer. And as we saw in Afghanistan, in liberation, they celebrate.

America has a greater objective than controlling threats and containing resentment. We will work for a just and peaceful world beyond the war on terror.

Other books by Thomas M. Freiling

Prayers to Move Your Mountains
(Thomas Nelson)

Reagan's God and Country
(Vine Books)

Abraham Lincoln's Daily Treasure
(Fleming H. Revell)

To contact the author, write:
10640 Main Street
Suite 204
Fairfax, VA 22030

or e-mail:
tfreiling@allegiancepress.com.